MICHAEL JACKSON'S
# MALT WHISKY
*Companion*

MICHAEL JACKSON'S
# MALT WHISKY
*Companion*

## A CONNOISSEUR'S GUIDE
## TO THE MALT WHISKIES
## OF SCOTLAND

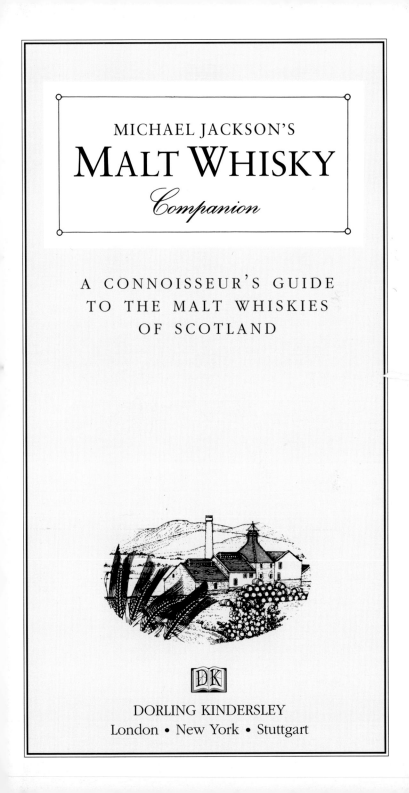

DK

**DORLING KINDERSLEY**
London • New York • Stuttgart

**DK**

A DORLING KINDERSLEY BOOK

**Editors**
Lisa Minsky, Roddy Craig

**Art editor**
Phil Kay

**Managing editor**
Jemima Dunne

**Managing art editor**
Tina Vaughan

Third edition first published in Great Britain in 1994 by
Dorling Kindersley Limited
9 Henrietta Street, London WC2E 8PS
Reprinted 1995 (twice), 1996 (twice), 1997

A CIP catalogue record for this book is
available from the British Library.

ISBN 0-7513-0146-9

Printed by Wing King Tong, Hong Kong

## New in this edition

Just as the lover of food and wine becomes familiar with single malts, and establishes a few favourites, a further group of seemingly new names and labels appears from the Highlands and Lowlands, the coasts and islands.

Every malt distillery in Scotland is discussed in this book, along with the handful in other countries that produce malt whisky. I have tried to include every current version – there are approximately 200 new or revised tasting notes in this edition – and I have also retained, where space permits, earlier versions and recent small-batch bottlings. The latter offer a snapshot of the moment and will be updated in future editions. These small-batch bottlings are intended for the enthusiast who might find them on the shelf in some corner of the world, and to give an impression of the variations in which any malt might manifest itself.

Many malts are now being offered at the strength they leave the cask. Several of these "cask-strength" malts are also new in this edition. So are some whiskies that have been matured in unusual casks.

Some of the distillery entries in this edition are truly new. A distillery called simply Speyside, established at the beginning of the 1990s, makes its debut in this edition with a very young bottling called Drumguish. So also do youthful distilleries such as Allt-á-Bhainne (established in 1975), Braes of Glenlivet (established in 1974) and Mannochmore (established in 1972). Another newcomer to this edition is Strathmill, which seems to have been first bottled in 1993, in a 1980 vintage, though the distillery was established in 1891.

Most of the distillery entries in this edition are represented by one or more new bottlings, for which there are tasting notes. In some instances this has necessitated the shortening of previous notes. I have also, in some cases, revised earlier notes to highlight qualities I have noticed as I have tasted certain whiskies over the years.

*Michael Jackson*

# ORIGINS OF THE SPIRIT

The wild yeasts of the atmosphere spontaneously cause fermentation of natural sugars. This produces alcohol – turning grapes into wine, and grain into beer. The art of distillation was used by mariners (to render sea water drinkable), alchemists, makers of perfumes, and eventually in the production of medicines and alcoholic drinks.

Distilling may have come from the Orient, via the Moors, to Spain and Europe. There is some evidence of distilling in Ireland at the beginning of this millennium. The first indisputable reference in Scotland is an entry of 1494 in the archives of the National Exchequer. It records the purchase of malt by Friar John Cor of Dunfermline (the former capital city) to make "acquavitae". In medieval times, much production of alcoholic drinks was in abbeys. They were the centres of communities, with their own inns, and were also centres of learning and science.

Acquavitae, "the water of life", indicated simply "spirits". This word, in various spellings, is found today in some Nordic countries, and the French "eau-de-vie" translates in the same way. Rendered in Irish- and Scottish-Gaelic, the term becomes "uisge beatha" or "usquebaugh", among other spellings. These Gaelic names, sounding to the English-speaker like "uishgi", were corrupted to "whisky".

*Landseer's* The Highland Whisky Still, *painted in the 1820s, captures the atmosphere of an early illegal still.*

Like the original vodkas and today's gins, the first Scottish distillates were flavoured with herbs and spices. By the mid-1700s, a distinction was made in Scotland between these flavoured spirits and "plain malt".

## How whisky is made

The original way to make whisky is to turn barley into malt, infuse it in water, ferment it into a form of beer (or "wine"), then distil it by the batch in a copper vessel shaped like a kettle or cooking pot. Malt whisky is still produced only in this way. In the mid-1800s, the blends of malt whiskies began to be leavened with a lighter style – made less expensively, from a variety of grains (not all malted) in a continuous process, using a column-shaped "patent" still. These unspecified grains may include unmalted barley, wheat or maize.

## The birth of blends

The Scots, with their mountainous country and long coastline, are a maritime nation of explorers, traders and engineers. Their pioneering travels have made blended Scotches, produced from both malt and "grain" whiskies, the most international of spirits.

Although some of the sites are surely earlier, the oldest of today's Scottish distilleries date from the 1700s. Many date from illegal stills, and others from farms. In the 1700s and early 1800s, production was small and irregular, and the notion of "brands" or trademarks was unknown in any industry. Whisky was sold by the cask to country grocers and wine merchants. Johnnie Walker was such a shopkeeper; George Ballantine another; the Chivas brothers were partners in a shop. These merchants dealt with lack of consistency or volume by creating their own house vattings, and these became brands. John Dewar, who went into the business in 1806, was the first person to sell branded whisky in bottles.

## The rediscovery of single malts

Scotland is still the world's biggest exporter of spirit drinks, but the success of blends, owned by a handful of large corporations, made the few independent distillers of malt whisky nervous. In the post-war period, Glenfiddich began to export its whisky as a single malt, first to England, and then, in the late 1960s and 70s, to the rest of the world. What seemed like a lone gamble became an inspiration to others. Blended Scotch is still dominant in volume, but single malts like Glenfiddich, The Glenlivet, Glenmorangie, The Macallan and Laphroaig have established themselves internationally.

# SINGLE MALT:
# THE APPELLATION

The term SINGLE has a very precise meaning. It indicates that all of the whisky in the bottle was made in the same distillery. It is the product of a single distillery and has not been blended with whisky from any other distillery.

The term MALT indicates the raw material. The whisky is made exclusively from malted barley and no other grain, sugar or fermentable material. It is infused with water, fermented with yeast and distilled in a pot-still.

There are 100-odd malt distilleries in Scotland. Their products are the only Malts that may be called SCOTCH. A whisky must be distilled and matured for at least three years in Scotland in order to bear that appellation. The term "Scotch" cannot be applied – but the term "Single-Malt Whisky" can – to examples made in Ireland, somewhat experimentally in North America, and in New Zealand and Japan. These countries, however, have only a handful of distilleries between them.

While most bottles of single malt contain a vatting of several production runs, some are filled from a single batch. Such a whisky is sometimes identified as a "Single/Single". This means that it is a single malt from a single barrel. A single barrel might fill fewer than 250 bottles.

The Glenfiddich is a true single malt, but also uses on its label the term "Pure Malt", as if to wear both belt and braces. This is perhaps foolish, as the singularity sounds to be diminished by the term "Pure". On the labels of some other products, the term "Pure" indicates that, while the content is all pure malt whisky, it may come from several distilleries. This is true of several minor brands, especially in export markets. Any importer, distributor or store-chain can create its own brand – let us say Glentammy – and fill its bottles with whichever malt whiskies are available and attractively priced. The contents of its bottles may vary from one year to the next. For that reason, these products are not reviewed in this book, though some are very acceptable and excellent value. Some countries with no malt distilleries buy whiskies from Scotland and vat them under a national label.

A minor and diminishing category is the "Vatted Malt". This type of malt whisky is made in exactly the same way, but with more commitment to a distinct character. Vatted malts are discussed on pages 258–259.

# WHY SINGLE MALTS DIFFER

While some spirits, such as gin and vodka, can be made anywhere without influence on flavour and require no costly ageing, single-malt whisky is one of those drinks that is formed by its environment, from the local water to the shape of the stills and the climate during maturation. Each single malt represents a place, which also often provides the name.

MALTING: Barley has to be partially germinated before it can release its fermentable sugars. It is soaked in water until it begins to sprout, then this is arrested by drying the grains over heat. This steeping and drying process is called "malting". Traditionally, the Scots dried their malt over a peat fire, which gives Scotch its characteristic smokiness. A proportion of peat is usually still burned during malting.

MASHING: To complete the conversion of starch into fermentable sugars, the malt (which has been milled after malting) is mixed with warm water in a vessel called a mash tun. The liquid drained off is known as "wort".

FERMENTATION: The sugars in the wort are now turned into alcohol during fermentation, which takes place with the addition of yeast, in a fermentation vessel.

DISTILLATION: This is the boiling of the fermented wort, in a pot-still. Because alcohol boils more rapidly than water, the spirit is separated as a vapour, and collected as it condenses back to alcohol.

*Germinating malt must be turned, left, to aerate the grains. In the mash tun, above, rotating "blades" churn the malt.*

# THE POT-STILL

Single malt is distilled in traditional vessels that resemble a copper kettle, or pot, with a chimney-like spout. These are known as pot-stills. Most other types of whisky are made in a more modern system: a continuous still, shaped like a column, known as a column-still.

Much of the flavour of the malt is retained in pot distillation because this old-fashioned system is inherently inefficient. A column system can distil more thoroughly, but that makes for a less flavourful spirit. Blended Scotch whiskies contain a proportion of pot-still malt, leavened with continuous- or column-still whisky made from cheaper, unmalted grains.

### The shape of the still

The flavour of the distillate is greatly influenced by the shape of a pot-still, in ways that are not wholly understood. An example concerns stills that are especially tall. Vapour condenses in the upper reaches of the still before it can escape, falls back, and is re-distilled. This produces a more refined, lighter spirit. A shorter still will produce a richer, creamier, oilier spirit. Between these extremes, there are countless sizes and shapes of pot-still. Every aspect of size, shape, and surface area seems to enter a new permutation into performance. Distillers are reluctant to change the shape or size when new stills are fitted, for fear of losing the character of their whisky.

Most malts are run through two linked pot-stills: the wash-still and the spirit-still. In one or two Lowland distilleries and in Ireland, a system of three pot-stills, "triple-distillation", is used.

*Glenmorangie's pot-stills,* left, *are the tallest in Scotland. The Macallan's stills,* above, *are the smallest on Speyside.*

# THE INFLUENCES OF LOCATION

The two spirits most often compared for their regionality are Cognac and single-malt Scotch. In Cognac, the regions of production are contiguous, stretch about 90 miles from one end to the other, and are all in flat countryside. The single malts spread over an area of about 280 miles from one end to the other, from the southern Lowlands to the northern Highlands, from mountain to shore, from the Western Isles to the Orkneys. Cognacs are usually blends, often from more than one region, while a single malt bears the character of just one distillery.

### Water

Producers of several types of drink talk in hushed tones of the importance of their water. Nowhere is it more genuinely significant than in single-malt Scotches. The water used in the single malts is usually not treated, and each distillery's supply has its own character.

The character of the water is influenced not only by the rock from which it rises (see page 14), but also by the land over which it travels to the distillery. For example, in the Highlands, much of the water used in distilling rises from granite and flows over peat. Water from a mountain stream that flows over rocks may pick up minerals on its journey, adding firmness and crispness to the finished whisky. Some distilleries have water that flows over peaty, mossy, reedy, ferny or (most often) heathery moorland. This may impart grassy or herbal characteristics. Heather recognizably adds floral and honeyish notes.

Some water flows over peat, and whiskies may gain their peatiness from this; other whiskies have a peaty flavour from the use of the fuel in malting, and some from both sources. The distance the water flows over peat will also be an influence as will the character of the peat.

Water may make its presence felt several times. It is used to steep the grains in the handful of distilleries that have their own maltings, and then again in the infusion that precedes fermentation and distillation. It may also be used to reduce slightly the strength of the spirit off the still before maturation. Some distillers feel they achieve a better maturation if the spirit is reduced in strength by a few percentage points. The distilleries that have their own bottling lines also use the local water to reduce the strength of the whisky at packaging. When a new distillery is planned, a reliable source of good water will be a prime criterion in the choice of a site.

## Rock

Some of the waters are believed to take several hundred years to filter through the mountains before emerging. In 1990, geologists Stephen Cribb and Julie Davison made a study of rock formations in Scotland's whisky regions, and compared them with tasting notes in books on the drink, principally this one. Their findings suggested that the similar tastes in certain whiskies produced near each other might in part be due to the similar rock from which the water rose. For example, in the Lowlands, the crisp, dry, Glenkinchie and Rosebank share the same carboniferous rock. The oldest rock is that which supplies water to the Bowmore and Bruichladdich distilleries on Islay, off the west coast of Scotland; it was formed about 600–800 million years ago, and seems to contribute an iron-like flavour. The granite of the Grampians is often credited with the typically soft-water character of the Speyside whiskies of eastern Scotland. In the north-east, sandstone may make for the firmer body of whiskies like Glenmorangie. Highly individualistic whiskies like Talisker and Clynelish turn out to be based on rock not shared with others.

*Like most Scottish distilleries, Glenturret is set against hills and, beyond them, mountains, which provide water.*

## Snow

The snow that covers the Highland peaks melts to provide water that seeps through fissures in the rock, then emerges into mountain streams before filling the reservoirs of maltings and distilleries. There is melted snow in most bottles of whisky. This is especially true where the Grampian Mountains form a ridge across the biggest land-mass of the Highlands, and small rivers like the Livet and Fiddich flow into the Spey on their way north to the great inlet known as the Moray Firth.

## Soil

The soil will affect not only the water but also the character of the peat. If malting is done at the distillery, local peat will be used in the kilning. The age of the peat deposits, and their degree of grass-root or heather character, will have its own influence on the whisky.

## Barley

Scotland grows some of the world's best barley for malting, and much of it is cultivated in whisky-producing areas, especially the Lowlands and the stretches where the Spey and other rivers flow over flat, very fertile land to reach the Moray Firth. This coastal rim can have surprisingly long summer days, and cool breezes, though the latter can strengthen worryingly at harvest time in late summer.

For many years, the local Golden Promise barley was favoured by maltsters and distillers. Its short straw stands up to the wind; it ripens early (in August); and it produces nutty, rich flavours. As the industry has grown, farmers have moved to varieties that give them more grain per acre, and distillers to varieties that yield more fermentable sugars – but these do not necessarily produce such delicious flavours.

When Macallan experimentally made one batch with Golden Promise and another with a higher-yield barley, the difference was startling. The lesser variety produced a whisky that was clearly thinner-tasting, "dusty" and almost metallic.

## Temperature

A cold location makes for low temperature spring waters. When very cold water is available for use in the coils that condense the spirit, and the ambient temperature is low, an especially rich, clean, whisky is produced. Distilleries in shaded mountain locations are noted for this characteristic. The oak casks used during the maturation of the whisky expand and contract according to the temperature. The greater the local extremes of temperature, the more this happens.

## Micro-climate

Although similar yeasts (of broadly the ale type) are used throughout the malt-distilling industry, each tun room (fermentation hall) produces its own characteristics. This may vary according to the material from which the fermenting vessels are made – wood perhaps harbouring its own resident microflora – but it is also influenced by the micro-climate in and around the distillery.

## Air

This is a very significant factor. As the casks "breathe", they inhale the local atmosphere. The more traditional type of maturation warehouse has an earth floor, and often a damp atmosphere. The influence of this is especially noticeable in distilleries that are close to the sea. Often, their maturation warehouses are at the water's edge, washed by high seas. Some single malts, especially those from rocky coasts, have a distinctly briny or seaweedy character.

# THE CLASSIC REGIONS

Like wines – and many other drinks – the single malts of Scotland are grouped by region. As with wines, these regions offer a guideline rather than a rule. Within Bordeaux, a particular Pomerol, for example, might have a richness more reminiscent of Burgundy; similar comparisons can be made in Scotland. The regions in Scotland, the Lowlands, the Highlands, Campbeltown and the island of Islay have their origins in the regulation of licences and duties, but they do also embrace certain characteristics.

## The Lowlands

This area tends to produce whiskies in which the softness of the malt itself is evident, untempered by Highland peatiness or coastal brine and seaweed. The Lowlands is defined by a line following old county boundaries and running from the Clyde estuary to the River Tay. The line swings north of Glasgow and Dumbarton and runs to Dundee and Perth.

## The Highlands

By far the biggest region, the Highlands inevitably embraces wide variations. The western part of the Highlands, at least on the mainland, has only a few, scattered, distilleries, and it is difficult to generalise about their character. If they have anything in common, it is a rounded, firm, dry character, with

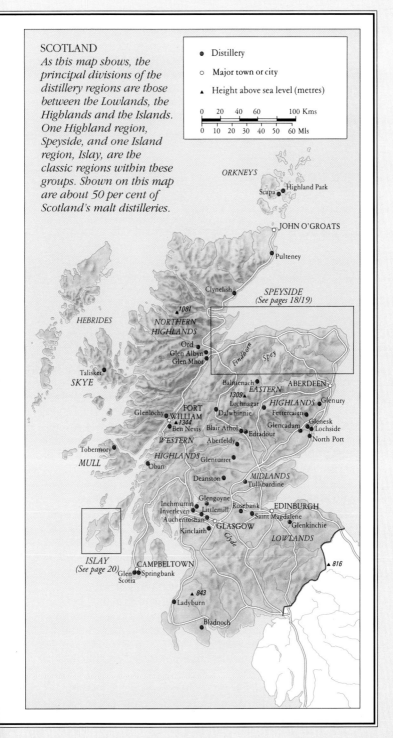

**SCOTLAND**

*As this map shows, the principal divisions of the distillery regions are those between the Lowlands, the Highlands and the Islands. One Highland region, Speyside, and one Island region, Islay, are the classic regions within these groups. Shown on this map are about 50 per cent of Scotland's malt distilleries.*

• Distillery

○ Major town or city

▲ Height above sea level (metres)

0    20    40    60         100 Kms
0   10   20   30   40   50   60 Mls

ORKNEYS

Scapa ● Highland Park

JOHN O'GROATS

● Pulteney

Clynelish ●

SPEYSIDE
(See pages 18/19)

HEBRIDES

▲ *1081*

NORTHERN
HIGHLANDS

Ord ●
Glen Albyn ●
Glen Mhor ●

*Findhorn*    *Spey*

Talisker ●

SKYE

Balmenach ● ABERDEEN ○

*1309* ▲ EASTERN

Glenlochy ● FORT
WILLIAM ○ Lochnagar ● HIGHLANDS ● Glenury
Dalwhinnie ● Fettercairn ●
▲ *1344*    Glencadam ● ● Glenesk
● Ben Nevis    Blair Athol ● ● Lochside
Edradour ● North Port ●

Tobermory ● WESTERN
Aberfeldy ●

MULL    HIGHLANDS

Oban ○ Glenturret ●

Deanston ● MIDLANDS
Tullibardine ●

Glengoyne ●
Inchmurrin ● Littlemill ● Rosebank ● EDINBURGH ○
Inverleven ● Saint Magdalene ●
Auchentoshan ● Glenkinchie ●
Kinclaith ● GLASGOW ○

LOWLANDS

*Clyde*

ISLAY
(See page 20)    CAMPBELTOWN ▲ *816*

Glen ● Springbank
Scotia

▲ *843*

● Ladyburn

Bladnoch ●

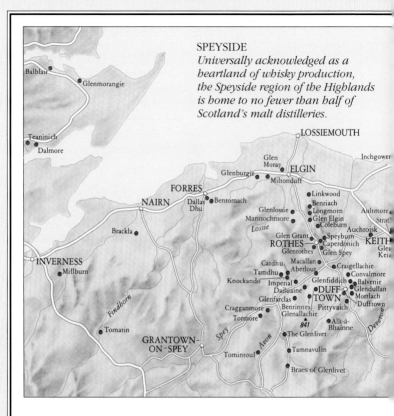

SPEYSIDE
*Universally acknowledged as a heartland of whisky production, the Speyside region of the Highlands is home to no fewer than half of Scotland's malt distilleries.*

Balblair
Glenmorangie

Teaninich
Dalmore

LOSSIEMOUTH

Glen Moray
Glenburgie
Miltonduff
ELGIN
Inchgower

FORRES
NAIRN
Dallas Dhu
Benromach
Glenlossie
Mannochmore
Lossie
Linkwood
Benriach
Longmorn
Glen Elgin
Coleburn
Aultmore
Strat'

Brackla
Glen Grant
Speyburn
Auchroisk
Caperdonich
ROTHES
Glenrothes
Glen Spey
KEITH
Glen
Kei

INVERNESS
Millburn
Findhorn
Cardhu
Tamdhu
Knockando
Imperial
Dailuaine
Glenfarclas
Cragganmore
Tormore
Macallan
Aberlour
Benrinnes
Glenallachie
841
The Glenlivet
Craigellachie
Convalmore
Glenfiddich
Balvenie
DUFF TOWN
Glendullan
Mortlach
Dufftown
Pittyvaich
Allt-à-Bhainne

Tomatin
GRANTOWN-ON-SPEY
Spey
Avon
Tomintoul
Tamnavulin
Deveron

Braes of Glenlivet

some peatiness. The far north of the Highlands has several whiskies with a notably heathery, spicy, character, probably deriving both from the local soil and the coastal location of the distilleries. The more sheltered East Highlands and the Midlands of Scotland (sometimes described as the South Highlands) have a number of notably fruity whiskies.

None of these Highland areas is officially regarded as a region, but the area between them, known as Speyside, is universally acknowledged as a heartland of malt distillation. This area, between the cities of Inverness and Aberdeen, sweeps from granite mountains down to fertile countryside, where barley is among the crops. It is the watershed of a system of rivers, the principal among which is the Spey. Although it is not precisely defined, Speyside is commonly agreed to extend at least from the River Findhorn in the west to the Deveron in the east.

Within this region are several other rivers, notably the Livet. The *Speyside* single malts are noted in general for their elegance and complexity, and often a refined smokiness. Beyond that, they have two extremes: the big, sherryish type,

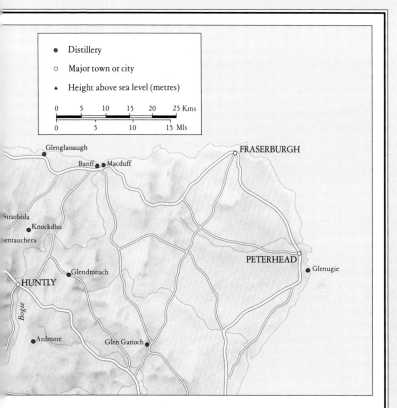

as typified by The Macallan, Glenfarclas and Aberlour; and the lighter, more subtle style. Within Speyside, the River *Livet* is so famous that its name is borrowed by some whiskies from far beyond its glen. Only one may call itself The Glenlivet, only Braes of Glenlivet and Tamnavulin are produced in the valley, and only Tomintoul in the parish. These are all delicate malts, and it could be more tentatively argued that other valleys have malts that share certain characteristics.

The Highland region includes a good few coastal and island malts, but one peninsula and just one island have been of such historical importance in the industry that they are each regarded as being regions in their own right.

## Campbeltown
On the peninsula called the Mull of Kintyre, on the west coast of Scotland, Campbeltown once had about 30 distilleries. Today, it has only two. One of these, Springbank, produces two different single malts. This apparent contradiction is achieved by the use of a lightly peated malt in one and a smokier kilning in the other. The Campbeltown single malts

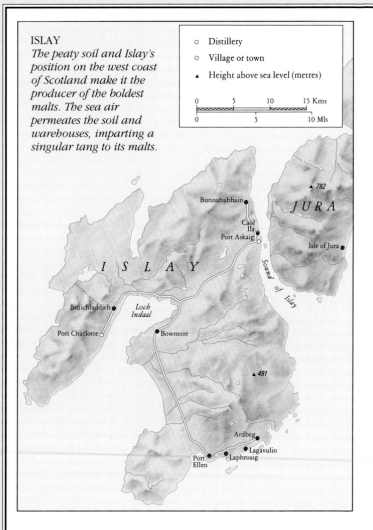

**ISLAY**
*The peaty soil and Islay's position on the west coast of Scotland make it the producer of the boldest malts. The sea air permeates the soil and warehouses, imparting a singular tang to its malts.*

○  Distillery
○  Village or town
▲  Height above sea level (metres)

0      5      10      15 Kms
0            5            10 Mls

Bunnahabhain•

*JURA*
▲ 782

Caol Ila
Port Askaig•

*Sound of Islay*

Isle of Jura•

*I S L A Y*

Bruichladdich•    *Loch Indaal*

Port Charlotte○        •Bowmore

▲ 491

Ardbeg•
•Lagavulin
Laphroaig
Port Ellen○

are very distinctive, with a briny character. Although there are only three of them, they are still considered by serious malt lovers to represent a region in their own right.

**Islay**
Pronounced "eye-luh", this is the greatest of whisky islands: much of it deep with peat, lashed by the wind, rain and sea in the Inner Hebrides. It is only 25 miles long, but has no fewer than eight distilleries, although not all are working. Its single malts are noted for their seaweedy, iodine-like, phenolic character. A dash of Islay malt gives the unmistakable tang of Scotland to many blended whiskies.

# MATURATION

Much has been learned through research in the 1990s about the influence of maturation on the aroma and flavour of whisky, but only in recent years has a scientific approach been developed. The production of whisky evolved empirically, and for years its magic was taken for granted.

Wooden casks were originally used simply as containers for the freshly distilled spirit, the ability of spirits to develop with age was appreciated later. Although the benefits of maturation are said to have been known earlier to wealthy cellar-owners, whisky was not systematically aged until the late nineteenth century.

### Choice of wood

Among the woods used in the production of alcoholic drinks, oak is by far the most widely favoured. It is strong, yet pliable, and makes excellent casks. In theory, all Scotch whisky is aged in oak. In practice, a cask made from chestnut or mahogany very occasionally turns up in a distillery. On the very rare occasions when this happens, no one can remember how the cask was acquired. Although cask acquisitions are monitored carefully today, this was not always the case. Most distilleries have thousands of casks, some acquired 50 or 60 years ago.

Scotland is a mountainous country with plenty of pines but few oaks, and in the early days, wood from England was used. Then the Scots began to take advantage of the English

*Oak staves are steamed and shaped into Bourbon casks,* above left. *These are briefly charred,* above right, *before being hand-finished.*

taste for sherry. In the heyday of that fashion, empty casks could be found in great quantity in the English port of Bristol, where merchants bottled sherry from Spain.

Not only were the casks inexpensive, they were found to impart a delicious richness and roundness to the whisky. One producer calls this "a sublime accident". This source of casks diminished when England's stately taste for sherry declined, and even more when Spain became a modern democracy and decided that the bottling of sherry in the growing areas would provide useful jobs for its citizens.

When sherry casks became hard to find, many distilleries moved to Bourbon barrels. The definition of "Bourbon whiskey" requires that it be aged in a new cask; as a robust, sweet, corn-based whiskey, it gains some of its typical character from the caramel flavours, vanillins and tannins in the wood. (Vanillins are a natural component of wood. Their flavours are similar to those of the vanilla pod). After one fill of Bourbon, such a cask imparts much more delicate flavours to a Scotch malt whisky.

Some distillers refer to new Bourbon barrels as "American oak", and most call a cask of any origin "plain wood" after a couple of fills of whisky. In the past, new wood may have been commonly used, but its flavours, while helpful to Bourbon, tend to overpower a whisky as complex as Scotch.

*The Macallan's production director samples sherry in a bodega; the casks labelled "MG" will be used to mature the Macallan malt.*

As drinks, both sherry and Bourbon have suffered some ups and downs in their popularity in recent years, and this means that the supply of wood from those sources cannot be guaranteed. Scottish distillers may again find themselves using substantial quantities of new wood in the future, but will seek means to restrain its influences on flavour.

Although each single malt comes from only one distillery, it is usually a vatting of several production runs. Most distilleries with "official" bottlings try to ensure some consistency in their product. Each bottling may contain an orchestration of whiskies from first- and second-fill sherry casks, first- and second-fill Bourbon barrels, and "plain wood", fine-tuned each time to achieve the desired end result.

### Other "woods"
Occasionally rum casks and port pipes have found their way into whisky warehouses. Springbank has released casks of a sweet, buttery, spicy, minty malt matured in rum casks. In 1993, Gordon and MacPhail released an aromatic, gingery, crisp, oaky malt, aged in a brandy cask, and a very toffeeish example from a port pipe. Both had been laid down in the 1960s. When Glenmorangie released its port-finished whisky in 1994 (see page 151), it also offered an experimental tasting of a very crisp (almost brittle) vintage aged in a Limousin cask intended for Cognac, and a toastier example matured in Madeira wood. These two were not launched into the market, but other versions may be.

### The effect of wood on maturation
Several processes take place during maturation. While the new distillate may have some harsh, "spirity" flavours, these can be lost by evaporation. With the expansion and contraction of the wood, caused by seasonal changes in temperatures, spirit flavours may be exhaled and the natural aromas of the environment taken into the cask: piney, seaweedy and salty "sea-air" characteristics can all be acquired in this way. Flavours are also imparted by the cask: sherry wood may add the nutty note of the wine; Bourbon barrels can impart caramel flavours, vanillins and tannins.

American oak is used in the production not only of all Bourbon barrels but also of many sherry casks. Spain also uses its own oak. American oak is finer grained, harder and slower to mature the whisky. Spanish oak is more resiny. The two oaks are from different families, the Spanish being accustomed to the maritime conditions of western Europe, the American to the inland environment of its continent.

## The importance of oxidation in maturation

Perhaps the most important influence on the flavour is that of a very slow, gentle, oxidation of the whisky. While oxygen is regarded as an "enemy" by brewers and some wine-makers, because it can cause "stale" flavours, its influence is also a part of the character of Madeira wines, for example. The importance of oxidation in the maturation of whisky has been the subject of much recent work by Dr Jim Swan, originally at the Pentlands Scotch Whisky Research Institute (which is owned by the industry), and more recently by his own company.

Dr Swan argues that oxidation increases the complexity and intensity of pleasant flavours in whisky, especially fragrant, fruity, spicy and minty notes. As in the production of all alcoholic drinks, the flavours emerge from a complex series of actions and reactions. Traces of copper from the stills are the catalyst. They convert oxygen to hydrogen peroxide, which attacks the wood, releasing vanillin. This promotes oxidation, and additionally pulls together the various flavours present. These processes vary according to the region of origin of the wood, and its growth patterns.

This has led distillers to concern themselves not only with the distinctions between sherry and Bourbon wood, and the country in which the trees grew, but also the region. In Spain, where most oak comes from Galicia, trees from mountainous districts are more resiny. In the United States, the growth is mainly in Ohio, Kentucky, Illinois, Missouri and Arkansas. The westerly part of this contiguous region has the poorest soil and the most arid climate, and there the trees have to fight to survive. This optimises spring growth, which has the most open texture and is the most active in the maturation process.

# ALCOHOL CONTENT/PROOF

Alcohol by volume is the easiest measure to understand, and the system that is now standard throughout Europe. Forty per cent alcohol by volume is the equivalent of 70 proof in the complicated system previously used in Britain, or 80 proof in the American system.

Malt whisky comes off the still at an average strength between the mid- or lower 70s and upper 60s, and may be reduced in strength by the addition of water to the mid-60s before being matured. During ageing, it may lose up to 2.5 per cent of its alcohol per year in evaporation. It will emerge from maturation at around 60 or in the upper 50s, depending upon the duration of ageing, but is customarily reduced further with water before being bottled.

# A-Z
# OF SINGLE MALTS

**O**ver the next 224 pages is a review, in alphabetical order, of every Scottish malt distillery that has ever seen its product in a bottle. There is now only the odd new distillery, such as Kininvie, that has not. Where a distillery's malts can be sampled in two or three different ages or strengths, I have made notes across the range. I have also given each example a score (see page 31).

### Malts of different ages
On all single malts, the age on the label represents the youngest whisky that is in the bottle. Some distilleries are introducing younger bottlings (often with no age statement) for consumers who wish to sample their product at a more competitive price. A competitively priced single malt with no age statement may contain whiskies of five years or less, and is unlikely to have any of more than ten years. Such a vatting is still a "single" malt, because all the whisky comes from one distillery.

There is also a growing market for more mature malts. Some distillers also offer highly priced single malts with no age statement, but with references to antiquity. These may well contain whiskies that are in the 12- to 18-year-old range. Such a balance of malts can be very attractive, but is undersold as a 12-year-old, yet cannot be called an 18-year-old.

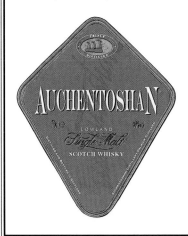

*A label that bears no age statement invites the consumer to speculate. The youngest malt whisky in the bottle may have something between five and eight years' maturation, though a proportion of the content may be much more mature.*

*"Flora and Fauna" from a mothballed distillery.*

*Vintage malts are unique to their year of bottling.*

## "Vintage" edition malts

When a distillery offers its whisky at a specific age, whether 10, 12, 18 or 25 years old, for example, it will vat together several production runs in order to ensure consistency. None will be younger than the age stated on the label, though some may be older. The idea is that a 12-year-old malt bottled two or three years ago should taste much the same as one of the same age packaged next week. Some labels, rather than showing an age, indicate a specific year. This is the year of production, and the buyer can assume that the whisky was aged until it was bottled. Often, the age of bottling is also shown, perhaps in smaller type. Many of the tasting notes in this edition represent new vintages.

## Similar labels

Many of the labels in this book are similar. One reason is that labels are similar in design because they represent malts packaged by independent bottlers (see pages 27–29). Another reason is that in 1990–91, United Distillers released a series of its whiskies that had previously not been available in "official" bottlings. Until that time, these whiskies had been used for blending, although some could be found in "unofficial" bottlings. United Distillers owns more distilleries than any other drinks company, so these new releases represented a considerable selection. All of these malts have labels depicting local flora and fauna, and are intended primarily for sale in the area of each distillery – though some have already been marketed nationally in Britain. I have dubbed them the "Flora and Fauna" series, though this is not an official designation.

# INDEPENDENT AND UNOFFICIAL BOTTLINGS

Without independent bottlers, many interesting malt whiskies would have vanished forever into blends, and would never be seen as singles. Only two distilleries, Glenfiddich and Springbank, have bottling lines on their premises. This is significant because in those two distilleries any reduction in strength at the bottling stage is done with the same water used in distillation. Many distilleries are owned by drinks companies that have their own central bottling lines. Others contract bottlers, or permit wine-and-spirit merchants to do the packaging and marketing for them. In these cases, the water used for reduction will be either filtered or de-natured.

It is unusual for a distiller to reserve all his whisky for bottling as a single malt. Most sell a substantial proportion of their output into the trade, via brokers, for blending. Some of this whisky finds its way into independent bottlings. For example, the owner of a distillery called McSporran may market some of his whisky under that name, but the McSporran legend will also be found on independent bottlings. These bottlings contain his whisky, but not necessarily at the age or strength he deems perfect, or from the casks he prefers.

Some distillers restrict supply of their whisky to try and stop independent bottlers, while other distillers resort to the law. Sometimes the independent bottlers vary the name slightly, to indicate the source without infringing a trademark.

### Small batch bottlings
Some independent bottlings are filled from just the odd cask, or a very small "parcel" of casks (the term employed in the industry). It is therefore possible that a particular malt discussed in this edition may no longer be available from the bottler. Yet the malt may be spotted on a shelf in a store or bar in Glasgow or London, Chicago or Tokyo, where it may take several years to be drained by the occasional customer.

### Gordon and MacPhail
This company still operates the licensed grocery store in Elgin with which its business began, but it is known by whisky-lovers everywhere for its activities as an independent bottler. Gordon and MacPhail, established in 1895, holds thousands of casks of whisky in stock, some of which date back half a

century. The company bottles some whiskies with the authority or tacit agreement of the distillers. Because of its considerable stocks, it can vat its bottlings to impart some level of consistency. Gordon and MacPhail bottles its rarer malts under the label "Connoisseurs Choice". Many of its whiskies are sherry-aged. Gordon and MacPhail's shop is at 58–60 South Street, Elgin (tel: 0343-545111).

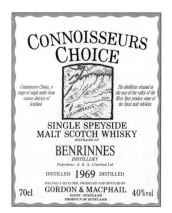

*Many distilleries feature as Connoisseurs Choices.*

*This Cadenhead bottling uses the old "Glenlivet" form.*

### William Cadenhead

This independent bottler has, in the past, printed its registered address in Aberdeen on its labels, but it is based in Campbeltown. Cadenhead shares premises and ownership with the Springbank distillery. The company has, over the years, collected an extraordinary selection of odds and ends, often in very small "parcels". Whiskies aged in unusual woods, or at odd strengths, or from unlikely sources, are forever emerging from Cadenhead. Many of the bottlings are at cask strength, and none are chill-filtered. (This process ensures clarity, but removes some of the flavour from the whisky. Most whiskies are chill-filtered.) Cadenhead's very plain, white-on-black label is now being replaced by a smarter buff one, with the trim colour-coded to indicate the region of origin of the whisky. Cadenhead retails through a whisky shop at 172 Canongate, on the Royal Mile, Edinburgh (tel: 031-556-5864), but wholesales from Campbeltown (tel: 01586-554258). Newly distilled spirit may be bought "en primeur" from Cadenhead, who will mature it in the cask until an appointed date, perhaps a 21st birthday.

## Other independent bottlers

*James MacArthur,* with a telephone number in High Wycombe, England (tel: 04945-30740), and Edinburgh-based *Signatory* (tel: 031-555-4988) have established reputations for interesting bottlings. Some bottlings are carried out by wine merchants such as *Berry Brothers and Rudd* in St James's, London; and companies like *Reid's* and *Avery's,* both of Bristol. Newer specialists in unusual bottlings include *The Whisky Connoisseur,* Thistle Mill, Station Road, Biggar, Scotland; *The Whisky Castle,* Tomintoul, Ballindalloch, Banffshire, Scotland; and *Inverallan,* in Alva, Scotland (also at 418 South 18th Street, Philadelphia, US). Prime Malt is a series name for a range of usually sherryish malts from *Carlton Importers* of Baltimore. *Michel Couvreur,* of Meldrum House, Aberdeenshire, offers a range of single-cask bottlings of varying character. There are a growing number of other independent labels, some available only in certain countries. Many of these are supplied by the bottlers mentioned above.

*Signatory is one of the newer independent labels, here offering a rare edition of the malt whisky from the Clynelish distillery.*

## Society bottlings

*The Scotch Malt Whisky Society,* The Vaults, Leith, Edinburgh (tel: 031-554-3452) pioneered cask-strength bottlings. These are offered to members in regular mailings, together with tasting notes.

*The Malt Whisky Association,* The Corn Exchange, The Pantiles, Tunbridge Wells, Kent, England (tel: 0892-513295) has its own bottlings under the name Master of Malt. There are a growing number of clubs and mail-order suppliers.

# A GUIDE TO THE TASTING NOTES

Whatever the arguments about their relative prices, no one denies that a Château Latour is more complex than a mass-market table wine. Even within the range of fine wine, such judgements can be made clearly enough. The fine wines of the whisky world are the single malts. Some malts are made to higher standards than others, and some are more distinctive than their neighbours. This cannot honestly be obscured by the producers' blustery arguments about "personal taste". Neither, though, can the excellence of such complex products be measured very satisfactorily.

Throughout this section, I have, as far as possible, given tasting notes for every malt currently available. A tasting note cannot be definitive, but it can be a useful guide: if you are looking for a light dry malt, do not choose this one, pick the next. If you wanted something rich and sherryish, here is the one. This is the spirit, so to speak, in which I have over the years attempted to describe the character of beer, and in this work, single-malt whisky. To provide as full a picture as possible, the introduction to each distillery finishes with a note of HOUSE STYLE, indicating the character in general of its whiskies. Individual examples are then given tasting notes, including COLOUR, NOSE, BODY, PALATE, and FINISH. Each malt is also rated with a score out of 100.

### House style
In my introductions to each distillery, I describe its particular house style and propose a moment for each malt. These suggestions are meant as an encouragement to try each in a congenial situation. They are not meant to be taken with excessive seriousness.

### Colour
The natural colour of a malt matured in plain wood is a very pale yellow. Darker shades, ranging from amber to ruby to deep brown, can be imparted by sherry wood. Some distilleries use casks that have been treated with concentrated sherry, and this can cause a caramel-like appearance and palate. I do not suggest that one colour is in itself better than another, though a particular subtle, or profound, hue can heighten the pleasure of a fine malt. It is, after all, a drink to contemplate.

## Nose

Some lovers of wines and spirits feel that single malts are unusual among drinks in the honesty of their aroma. This school says that, in malts, the nose gives an accurate indication of the palate. I do not agree. In my perception, characteristics in the nose can move into the background of the palate, then re-emerge in the finish.

## Body

Lightness or fullness might be required on different occasions, but body and texture (sometimes known as "mouth feel") are distinct features in the overall character of each malt.

## Palate

In the enjoyment of any complex drink, each sip will offer new aspects of the taste. Even one sip will gradually unfold a number of taste characteristics in different parts of the mouth over a period of, say, a minute. This is notably true of single malts. Some present a very extensive development of palate. A taster working with an unfamiliar malt may go back to it several times over a period of days, in search of its full character. I have adopted this technique in my tastings for this book.

## Finish

In all types of alcoholic drink, the "finish" is a part of the experience. In some drinks, including most single malts, it is more than a simple aftertaste, however important that may be. It is a crescendo, followed by a series of echoes. When I leave the bottle, I like to be whistling the tune.

## Score

The scoring system I have developed and used in the A-Z section is intended as a guide to the status of the malts. Each tasting note is given a numerical score out of 100. Of these scores, one in the 50s indicates, in my view, a malt lacking in balance or character, and which – in fairness – was probably never meant to be bottled as a single. The 60s suggest an enjoyable but unexceptional malt. Anything in the 70s, especially beyond 75, is well worth tasting. The 80s are distinctive and exceptional. The 90s are the greats.

# ABERFELDY

**Producer** United Distillers
**Region** Highlands **District** Midlands

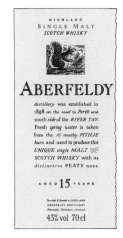

**L**OVERS OF DEWAR'S may recognise this as its signature malt. The hard water rises from whinstone flecked with iron and gold, and runs through pine, spruce, birch and bracken. The slowly run stills make a clean, strong spirit. The handsome distillery itself, built in 1896 and expanded in the 1960s and 1970s, overlooks the Tay Valley from the Grampian hill resort and market town of Aberfeldy, in raspberry-growing country.

**House style** Firm, oily, fruity. After dinner or book-at-bedtime.

---

**ABERFELDY 15-year-old, 43 vol, Flora and Fauna**

**Colour** Amber.

**Nose** Oil, incense, heather, lightly piney and peaty.

**Body** Medium.

**Palate** Very full flavours. Light peat, barley, fresh, clean, touches of Seville orange, rounded.

**Finish** Sweetness moves to fruitiness, then to firm dryness.

**SCORE 77**

---

### Other versions of Aberfeldy

Gordon and MacPhail's Connoisseurs Choice versions have fractionally less distillery character and more sherry. A 1970 was superseded by a maltier '74, and now by a delicious '75 that seems much richer and bigger all round. SCORE 76.

# ABERLOUR

**Producer** Pernod/Campbell Distillers
**Region** Highlands   **District** Speyside

T HE VILLAGE OF ABERLOUR lies in the heart of Speyside malt-distilling country. The distillery, called simply Aberlour, probably pre-dates its official recognition in 1826. It was expanded in 1945, on its purchase by Campbell Distillers, now owned by Pernod Ricard.

Settlement in the area dates to the time of St Dunstan, who, in the seventh century, baptised converts at a local spring. Aberlour uses the soft spring water that rises from the granite mountain, Ben Rinnes. Aberdeenshire peat is lightly employed. Between 25 and 50 per cent of the spirit is matured in sherry casks, the rest in Bourbon wood, and they are married for a time. Aberlour pioneered the sale of whisky en primeur, and collaborated with the Austrian designer Georg Riedel in the creation of a special glass for single malts.

**House style** Soft, medium to heavy, nutty, spicy (nutmeg?), sherry-accented. After dinner.

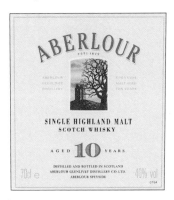

| ABERLOUR 10-year-old, 40 vol |
|---|
| **Colour** Amber. |
| **Nose** Full, malty, spicy, mint-toffee. |
| **Body** Remarkably soft and smooth. Medium to full. |
| **Palate** Distinctively clinging mouth-feel, with long-lasting flavour development. Dry, cookie-like notes, malty sweetness, mint, nutmeg and berry-fruit. |
| **Finish** Lingering, smooth, aromatic, clean. |

### SCORE 83

**ABERLOUR Antique, no age statement, 43 vol**

**Colour** Amber.

**Nose** Deeper, more sherry.

**Body** Firmer.

**Palate** More dryness, cookie-like toffee notes and spiciness.

**Finish** More robust and spicy, with hints of peat.

SCORE 84

**ABERLOUR, no age statement (100 proof)**

**Colour** Amber.

**Nose** Hint of oak.

**Body** Crisper.

**Palate** Dry oiliness, much more spiciness, some butterscotch.
Opens up considerably with a drop of water.

**Finish** Big, firm, dry.

SCORE 84

**ABERLOUR 1970, 43 vol**

**Colour** Amber.

**Nose** Mature, complex, with finesse.

**Body** Firm, smooth.

**Palate** Flavours beautifully combined. Oaky sappiness seems
to bring back some sweet maltiness.

**Finish** Smooth, complex, with some oakiness, and very long.

SCORE 85

# ALLT-A-BHAINNE

**Producer** Seagram/Chivas
**Region** Highlands  **District** Speyside (Fiddich)

N GAELIC, Allt-á-Bhainne means "the milk burn", and the distillery lies to the west of the River Fiddich in the foothills of Benrinnes, near Dufftown. One of the newer malt distilleries, it is housed in a handsome, tile-hung building commissioned in 1975 to supply malt whisky as a component of the blend Chivas Regal, and it was expanded in 1989. Had Chivas decided from the start to reserve some of the output for bottling as a single, it would have reached a sufficient age in the late 1980s. So far, this has not been done, but casks sold to brokers or blenders have given rise to some independent bottlings from the early 1990s

**House style** Fragrant (dried flowers?), light. Aperitif.

---

**ALLT-A-BHAINNE The Castle Collection, 13-year-old, 43 vol**

| Colour Pale gold. |
|---|

**Nose** Hint of peat. Flowery sweetness, becoming slightly sticky.

**Body** Light but firm.

**Palate** Light, sweetish start, a little bland, but developing flowery and spicy notes.

**Finish** Light, flowery-spicy, pleasant.

### SCORE 73

**Other versions of Allt-á-Bhainne**
A 12-year-old from James MacArthur seemed slightly bigger, no doubt as a result of the cask used. SCORE 74. A 1980 released by Oddbins in 1992 seemed to have enjoyed sherry but was perhaps a little overwhelmed by the sappiness of the oak. SCORE 73.

# ARDBEG

**Producer** Allied Distillers
**Region** Islay    **District** South shore

I T IS THE EARTHINESS of Ardbeg, its gusts of peat smoke, leafy bonfires and tar, that make it the most traditional of island whiskies. The distillery may have its origins as far back as 1794, and was definitely operating by 1817. An influence in the character of Ardbeg's whiskies has been its own maltings, which were unusual in the fact that there were no fans, causing the peat smoke to permeate the grains very heavily. A 10-year-old distilled in 1983 and bottled in 1993 can still be found, but it is the last from that maltings. Ardbeg ceased production until 1989, when it reopened without its maltings. When post-1989 whisky comes onto the market, it will probably begin without an age statement. Whether it will have as hefty a character remains to be seen.

**House style** Earthy, smoky, salty, robust. A bedtime malt.

ESTABLISHED 1815

Ardbeg
FINEST
ISLAY SINGLE MALT
SCOTCH WHISKY
Guaranteed 10 years old
ARDBEG DISTILLERY LIMITED
ISLE OF ISLAY ARGYLL SCOTLAND
75 cl    40% vol

| ARDBEG 10-year-old, 40 vol |
| --- |
| **Colour** Fino sherry. |
| **Nose** Smoke, brine, iodine dryness. |
| **Body** Only medium to full, but very firm. A light heavyweight with a punch worthy of a higher division. |
| **Palate** Skips sweetly along at first, then becomes mean and moody in the lengthy middle of the encounter. |
| **Finish** Hefty, lots of iodine. |

### SCORE 85

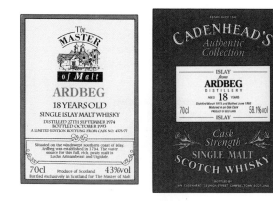

### ARDBEG 18-year-old, 43 vol, Master of Malt

**Colour** Gold.

**Nose** Fragrant, with seaweed and a hint of oak.

**Body** Medium to full, smooth.

**Palate** Sweetish, developing to seaweed and salt.

**Finish** Soothing, long, appetising.

### SCORE 90

### ARDBEG 18-year-old, 58.1 vol, Cadenhead

**Colour** Pale gold.

**Nose** Seaweedy, sweet and sour.

**Body** Medium to full, with some viscosity.

**Palate** Sweeter, maltier, then flavours reminiscent of edible seaweed and intense salt.

**Finish** Salty, tidal, attacking.

### SCORE 91

### ARDBEG 1974, 40 vol, Connoisseurs Choice

**Colour** Full gold to pale amber.

**Nose** Seaweed, oak.

**Body** Medium to full, smooth.

**Palate** Oakiness, sappiness, smokiness, sweetness, light touches of seaweed and salt.

**Finish** Perfumy, oaky.

### SCORE 88

**Other versions of Ardbeg**

For the moment, an unusually wide variety of ages and strengths of this malt can be found from several independent bottlers. There have also been good versions from the Scotch Malt Whisky Society and from some wine merchants and supermarket chains.

# ARDMORE

**Producer** Allied Distillers
**Region** Highlands    **District** Speyside (Bogie)

**S**OME OF THE NOTABLE maltiness of the Teacher's blends derives from this malt whisky. The distillery lies on the eastern fringes of Speyside, between the River Bogie, the Clashindarroch Forest and the foothills of the Grampians. It was erected by Teacher's in 1898 and despite expansion it has not lost its steam engine and coal-fire stills. The owners authorise Gordon and MacPhail to make bottlings, and there are other versions from independents.

**House style** Malty, creamy, robust. After dinner.

---

### ARDMORE 1977, 40 vol, Gordon and MacPhail

**Colour** Full gold, with amber tinge.

**Nose** Sherry, cream, cereal grains.

**Body** Oily, smooth.

**Palate** Tightly interlocking sweetness and dryness, cereal-grain character and fruitiness. Pears in cream, with a dash of sweet sherry.

**Finish** Cereal-grain, malty dryness.

SCORE 70

### ARDMORE 12-year-old, 56.2 vol, James MacArthur

**Colour** Full gold, bright.

**Nose** Fruity-sweet, malty, slightly spirity, powerful.

**Body** Soft, oily, drying in finish.

**Palate** Very sweet, malty, cedary, with some flowering currant.

**Finish** Softer, dry, with a late burst of warmth.

SCORE 67

# AUCHENTOSHAN

**Producer** Morrison Bowmore
**Region** Lowlands   **District** Western Lowlands

**C**LASSIC STATUS HAS surely by now been earned by these definitively Lowland malts, made by the region's traditional triple-distillation method. They are very light, certainly, but that is the Lowland style. Nor does lightness mean lack of character. In their own quiet way, these are well-defined single malts, with plenty of complexity. If you fancy single malts, but do not care for intensity, Auchentoshan offers the perfect answer: subtlety. The name is pronounced "Och'n'tosh'n", as though it were an imprecation. The distillery is just outside Glasgow, hidden in a hollow between the Clyde and the Kilpatrick Hills. It was founded around 1800, largely rebuilt after the Second World War, and re-equipped in 1974. A decade later, it was acquired by a private company, Stanley P. Morrison, providing a Lowland partner for their Islay and Highland distilleries, Bowmore and Glen Garioch. The company is now called Morrison Bowmore, and a minority stake is held by Suntory of Japan.

**House style** Light, citrussy, oily. Aperitif or restorative.

AUCHENTOSHAN, no age statement, 40 vol

**Colour** Greeny-gold.

**Nose** Oily, with hints of lemon zest.

**Body** Light, but with some oily mouth feel.

**Palate** Lemon-grass notes. Lightly sweet without being sticky.

**Finish** Light, crisp, quick.

SCORE 79

## AUCHENTOSHAN 10-year-old, 40 vol

**Colour** Bright gold, with greenish tinge.

**Nose** Saddlery, linseed oil, lemon zest.

**Body** soft, oily.

**Palate** Lemon grass, zest of lemon, citrussy, orangey. Sweetness without being sticky.

**Finish** Gingery, crisp, dryish, lightly warming.

### SCORE 85

## AUCHENTOSHAN 21-year-old, 43 vol

**Colour** Full, deep gold.

**Nose** Orange zest, date boxes, cedar, oil.

**Body** Light to medium, oily, very smooth indeed.

**Palate** Oily, citrussy, orange peel, lightly spicy, with lots of flavour development. Full of subtleties. More oak character than previous entry. Fresh, with no obtrusive woodiness.

**Finish** Cedar, vanilla, beautifully rounded and aromatic.

### SCORE 86

### Other versions of Auchentoshan
The Auchentoshan 12-year-old at 40 vol was more rounded than the 10-year-old, with a deft balance of freshness and maturity. SCORE 86. An 18-year-old at 43 vol was fuller, with a hint of linseed and surprising depth. SCORE 86. The 1966 at 43 vol had linseed again, although a little drier and with lots of flavour development. SCORE 86.

# AULTMORE

**Producer** United Distillers
**Region** Highlands **District** Speyside (Isla)

A FINE MALT IN THE OAKY style that seems to characterise the whiskies made near the River Isla. This distillery, which is just north of Keith, was built in 1896 and reconstructed in 1971. The malt whisky is a component of Dewar's and the Robert Harvey blends. Bottlings of Aultmore single malt, with the subtitle "Proprietors John and Robert Harvey and Co.", have been on the market for some years. In 1991, the parent company, United Distillers, added a bottling with a label in their "Flora and Fauna" series. Both are 12-year-olds, and similar in character. However, the Robert Harvey bottlings seem drier. Aultmore is perhaps best before dinner, although not every taster agrees. Like one of the bigger fino sherries, it is both appetising and relatively hefty.

**House style** Dry, herbal, spicy, oaky. Before dinner.

### AULTMORE 12-year-old, 40 vol

**Colour** Very pale.

**Nose** Big bouquet, fresh, warm and drily perfumed.

**Body** Firm.

**Palate** Light and fruity, developing hints of gentian or quinine.

**Finish** Crisp, very dry.

SCORE 75

**AULTMORE 12-year-old, 43 vol, Flora and Fauna**

**Colour** Very pale.

**Nose** Flowery, fresh, drily perfumed.

**Body** Medium, firm.

**Palate** Begins with a delicate, fruity-perfumy sweetness, developing to a flowery dryness.

**Finish** Delicate, dry, extraordinarily appetising.

SCORE 75

**AULTMORE 13-year-old, 46 vol, Cadenhead**

**Colour** Pale golden.

**Nose** Drier, with a hint of smoke.

**Body** Firm.

**Palate** Dry, flowery and expressive.

**Finish** Very dry.

SCORE 75

# BALBLAIR

**Producer** Allied Distillers
**Region** Highlands **District** Northern Highlands

THE DRY SPICINESS of the Northern Highland malts is present in definite but delicate form in the various versions of Balblair, which are made using water that has flowed in streams over crumbly local peat. From Ben Dearg, the waters flow into the River Carron and thence to the Dornoch Firth and the sea. A burn near the distillery feeds Balblair, which lies in peaty, low-lying land amid fields of sheep at Edderton, near the Firth. There is said to have been brewing and distilling in the vicinity in the mid-1700s. The first distillery was built in 1790, and the present building dates from the 1870s. The Balblair whisky is a component of the Ballantine's blends. Allied authorises Gordon and MacPhail to bottle Balblair as a single malt.

**House style** Light, firm, dry. Aperitif.

**BALBLAIR 5-year-old, 40 vol**
Balblair is regarded as a fast-maturing whisky, but the 5-year-old might be just too youthful for some malt-lovers. Nonetheless, it has a good following in the important Italian market.

| | |
|---|---|
| **Colour** | White wine. |
| **Nose** | Fresh, slightly sharp and pear-like. |
| **Body** | Light. |
| **Palate** | Clove-like spiciness. |
| **Finish** | Lingers, but not long enough. |

SCORE 70

**BALBLAIR 10-year-old, 40 vol, Gordon and MacPhail**

**Colour** Fuller than the 5-year-old.

**Nose** The fruitiness has become softer and more fragrant.

**Body** More texture.

**Palate** Hints of tart, fresh raspberries, becoming sweeter.

**Finish** Much longer. Drys out to an olive-like finish.

SCORE 76

**BALBLAIR 1964, 40 vol, Gordon and MacPhail**

**Colour** Gold.

**Nose** More intense than the 10-year-old.

**Body** Light, smooth.

**Palate** More sweetness and intensity, with a dash of fino sherry.

**Finish** Very dry.

SCORE 76

**BALBLAIR 1957, 40 vol, Gordon and MacPhail**

**Colour** Gold.

**Nose** On the woody side, has dried out a lot.

**Body** Light, firm.

**Palate** Full, dry, with a spicy peatiness.

**Finish** Crisp.

SCORE 74

*The hills that provide the water, the peaty land, the pagoda of the (retired) maltings...Balblair presents the classic picture of a Scottish whisky distillery in its pastoral setting.*

# BALMENACH

**Producer** United Distillers
**Region** Highlands   **District** Speyside

SPEYSIDE
SINGLE MALT
*SCOTCH WHISKY*

Sometime in the early 19th, after *walking*
in the *CROMDALE* hills *with*
his 2 *BROTHERS*, *James M^cGregor* settled
and established

## BALMENACH

*distillery. Spring water* from beneath those
*same HILLS* is still used to produce
this *RICH flavoured single MALT SCOTCH
WHISKY* of *exemplary* quality.

AGED **12** YEARS

43% vol   Distilled & Bottled in SCOTLAND   70cl
BALMENACH DISTILLERY, Cromdale, Morey, Scotland

**B**ALMENACH NESTLES IN hilly countryside between the upper reaches of the Spey and the Avon. The distillery, which officially dates from 1824, has contributed to many blends, including Crabbie's. Its first official bottling as a single malt came in 1991, but two years later United Distillers announced that the distillery was to be mothballed.

**House style** Very big, flowery, earthy. After dinner.

---

**BALMENACH 12-year-old, 43 vol, Flora and Fauna**

| |
|---|
| **Colour** Rich amber-red. |
| **Nose** Huge and deep. Pungent sherry character. Honeyish heather notes. |
| **Body** Medium to full. Soft and exceptionally smooth. |
| **Palate** Sherryish but dry. Alive with flavours: honey, ginger, bitter herbs, sappy, leafy notes. |
| **Finish** Rounded and satisfying. |

> SCORE 77

**Other versions of Balmenach**

James MacArthur 11-year-old, with no sherry, had a soft and flowery nose and astonishingly syrupy body, with a medium-dry maltiness of palate. SCORE 79. A Cadenhead 12-year-old was similar but even more flowery and a touch harsh on the finish. SCORE 78. A Connoisseurs Choice 1973 had less sherry than the official version, but was similar in style. SCORE 77.

# THE BALVENIE

**Producer** William Grant & Sons
**Region** Highlands **District** Speyside (Dufftown)

**N**EXT DOOR TO GLENFIDDICH, in Dufftown. The Balvenie was founded in 1892 and is owned by the same family company, but the whisky has quite a different style. The distillery uses barley from the family farm, has its own floor maltings, and its stills have a distinctive bulbous shape.

In 1993 the company dispensed with its brandy-flask-shaped bottles and increased the number of official versions from two to three. The shape of the bottles had sought to assert the status of malt whisky, but perhaps such stratagems are no longer necessary. Further to the Founder's Reserve that is still produced, a Single Barrel Edition and the 12-year-old Double Wood have been introduced. The last has maturation similar to an earlier Balvenie Classic. At one stage there was also a Classic 18-year-old with no sherry finish.

**House style** The most honeyish of malts, with a distinctively orangey note. Luxurious. After dinner.

**THE BALVENIE Founder's Reserve, 10-year-old, 40 vol**
(90 per cent American oak; 10 per cent sherry)

| |
|---|
| **Colour** Bright gold. |
| **Nose** Faintly musky orange-honey perfume. |
| **Body** Medium. |
| **Palate** Honeyed sweetness drying to lightly spicy notes. Just a touch of sherry. |
| **Finish** A surge of flavours, with lingering, syrupy honey. |

SCORE 85

## THE BALVENIE Double Wood, 12-year-old, 40 vol
(First- and second-fill Bourbon casks, then 6 to 12 months in sweet oloroso casks)

**Colour** Amber.

**Nose** Sherry and orange skins.

**Body** Medium, rich.

**Palate** Beautifully combined flavours; nutty, sweet, sherry, orangey fruitiness and cinnamon spiciness.

**Finish** Long, tingling, warm.

### SCORE 87

## THE BALVENIE Single Barrel Edition, 15-year-old, 50.4 vol
(All first-fill Bourbon casks)

**Colour** Pale gold.

**Nose** Assertive, dry, oak, cedar, heather-honey.

**Body** Firm.

**Palate** Lively. Orange-skins, sweetness and tartness.

**Finish** Cinnamon, ginger, pepper.

### SCORE 86

# BANFF

**Producer** United Distillers
**Region** Highlands    **District** Speyside (Deveron)

T HE HOUSE OF COMMONS was once supplied with whisky from this small distillery. It operated in the town whose name it bears, on the coast to the west of the mouth of the River Deveron. Established in 1824, rebuilt on a different site in 1863, and again in 1877, it was damaged by a bomb in the Second World War and has been the subject of much folk history. None of this prevented it from being closed and dismantled by its owners (then the Distillers Company Limited) in 1983. The whisky was used in the Slater Rodger blends. It was never generally available as a single malt, although it has appeared in independent bottlings.

**House style** Smoky, sweet, gingery. Restorative or after dinner.

---

**BANFF 1974, 40 vol, Connoisseurs Choice**

**Colour** Full, golden.

**Nose** Pleasantly smoky aroma.

**Body** Medium.

**Palate** Clean, assertive and smoky-sweet.

**Finish** Clean, gingery.

SCORE 66

# BEN NEVIS

**Producer** Nikka/Ben Nevis Co.
**Region** Highlands   **District** West Highlands

**O**FFICIAL BOTTLINGS of this malt have been long awaited. They are now available, albeit sporadically and in limited vintages. As might be expected, the distillery has found some good casks to bottle, much better than the odd ones with which independents have had to make do. The distillery at Fort William lies at the foot of Scotland's highest mountain, Ben Nevis (1,344m/4,409ft). The peak does not have quite the significance of Fuji, but it is a powerful symbol of Scotland. The distillery was established in 1825 by "Long John" McDonald. He gave rise to the brand name "Long John", now owned by Allied. Like many distilleries, it has had its ups and downs, but its manager Alex Ross has given it new life since its acquisition by Nikka of Japan. It provides a good, old-fashioned West Highland whisky.

**House style** Malty, robust, a touch of smoke. Restorative or book-at-bedtime.

DISTILLED AND BOTTLED IN SCOTLAND

**BEN NEVIS**

**SINGLE HIGHLAND MALT SCOTCH WHISKY**

BEN NEVIS DISTILLERY (FORT WILLIAM) LIMITED
DISTILLED IN 1972

75cl                              55.6% vol

| BEN NEVIS 1972, 55.6 vol |
| --- |
| **Colour** Gold, with an amber tinge. |
| **Nose** Sweet, waxy start (some tasters have been reminded of sweet peppers), then smoky. |
| **Body** Big, firm. |
| **Palate** Big, very malty, chocolatey, toffeeish. |
| **Finish** Chewy, robust, peaty, dry. |

SCORE 76

DISTILLED AND BOTTLED IN SCOTLAND

# BEN NEVIS

SINGLE HIGHLAND MALT
## SCOTCH WHISKY

BEN NEVIS DISTILLERY (FORT WILLIAM) LIMITED
**DISTILLED IN 1966**

75cl　　ウイスキー　　59%vol

**BEN NEVIS 26-year-old (1966), 59 vol**

**Colour** Amber.

**Nose** Some floweriness, malty, smoky.

**Body** Big, rounded.

**Palate** Smokiness, malt, sherry, oak.

**Finish** Robust, oaky.

SCORE 78

ESTABLISHED 1842

CADENHEAD'S
*Authentic Collection*

— HIGHLAND —
*from*
**BEN NEVIS**
DISTILLERY
AGED 15 YEARS
Distilled December 1977 and Bottled October 1993
Matured in an Oak Cask
PRODUCT OF SCOTLAND
70cl　　60.9% vol
— HIGHLAND —

*Cask Strength*
SINGLE MALT
SCOTCH WHISKY

BOTTLED BY
WM CADENHEAD · 32 UNION STREET CAMPBELTOWN SCOTLAND

**BEN NEVIS 15-year-old, 60.9 vol, Cadenhead**

**Colour** Gold.

**Nose** Floweriness and smokiness, both light.

**Body** Big, soft.

**Palate** Malty and sweet.

**Finish** Sweet, touches of estery fruitiness (mandarin?).

SCORE 69

# BENRIACH

**Producer** Seagram/Chivas
**Region** Highlands   **District** Speyside (Lossie)

BENRIACH DISTILLERY
EST. 1898
A SINGLE
**PURE HIGHLAND MALT**
Scotch Whisky
Benriach Distillery, in the heart of the Highlands, still malts its own barley. The resulting whisky has a unique and attractive delicacy
PRODUCED AND BOTTLED BY THE
**BENRIACH**
DISTILLERY C⁰
ELGIN, MORAYSHIRE, SCOTLAND, IV30 3SJ
Distilled and Bottled in Scotland
AGED 10 YEARS

**T**HE BETTER-KNOWN Longmorn is next door and under the same ownership, but Benriach now has the chance to establish itself: in 1994, it became available in its first official bottling as a single malt. Both distilleries were built in the 1890s, and extended in the 1960s and 1970s, and each contributes to the Chivas Regal blend.

**House style** Cookie-like, with touches of butterscotch. Restorative; a mid-afternoon malt?

| BENRIACH 10-year-old, 43 vol |
|---|
| **Colour** Pale gold. |
| **Nose** Honeyish, flowery. |
| **Body** Light, textured. |
| **Palate** Pronounced cereal-grain, slightly cookie-like in the middle, and a touch of butterscotch. |
| **Finish** Very flowery and well-defined. |

### SCORE 70

**Other versions of Benriach**
Connoisseurs Choice has two ages. A 1982 had a fuller gold colour and a perfumy, cereal-grain sweetness. SCORE 75. A 1976 had a yet fuller colour, and a dense, oily palate, with a touch of smoke. SCORE 76.

# BENRINNES

**Producer** United Distillers
**Region** Highlands   **District** Speyside

**B**EN RINNES (840m/2,759ft) is the dominant peak among the mountains overlooking the heart of Speyside. It gives its name to a distillery, Benrinnes, which may have been founded as early as the 1820s and was largely rebuilt in the 1950s. It had a long association with the Crawford blends. Its malt whisky, made by an unusual system of partial triple distillation, had its first official bottling in 1991.

**House style** Big, creamy, flavoursome. Restorative or after dinner.

SPEYSIDE
SINGLE MALT
*SCOTCH WHISKY*

## BENRINNES

*distillery* stands on the
*northern shoulder of BEN RINNES*
700 feet above *sea level*.
It is ideally located to exploit
the *natural advantages* of the
area-pure *air, peat* and
*barley* and the *finest* of *hill* water,
which rises through *granite*
from *springs* on the *summit*
of the *mountain*. The resulting
*single MALT SCOTCH WHISKY*,
is *rounded* and *mellow*.

A G E D **15** Y E A R S

Distilled & Bottled in *SCOTLAND*.
**BENRINNES DISTILLERY**
Aberlour, Banffshire, Scotland.

43% vol 70cl

---

**BENRINNES 15-year-old, 43 vol, Flora and Fauna**

**Colour** Autumnal reddish-brown.

**Nose** Heavy, almost creamy. A whiff of sherry, then a firm, smoky, burnt-toffee character.

**Body** Medium to full, firm.

**Palate** Dry, assertive, rounded. Flavours are gradually unlocked. Hints of licorice, aniseed, vanilla, bitter chocolate, smokiness.

**Finish** Satisfying, soothing. Faintly sweet and smoky.

SCORE 79

**BENRINNES 19-year-old, 50.2 vol, Cadenhead**

**Colour** Golden brown (toast-like).

**Nose** Heavy, creamy, oily, slatey.

**Body** Medium to full, smooth.

**Palate** Firm, complex. Oily-creamy.

**Finish** Drier with age. Licorice, rootiness. Long.

SCORE 79

**BENRINNES 1969, 40 vol, Connoisseurs Choice**

**Colour** Amber.

**Nose** Big, flowers-and-cream.

**Body** Medium, firm smooth.

**Palate** Light but creamy and toffeeish.

**Finish** Robust and dry, with a hint of smokiness.

SCORE 78

# BENROMACH

**Producer** United Distillers
**Region** Highlands   **District** Speyside (Findhorn)

 DELICIOUS MALT from a distillery that ceased production in 1983. Benromach is at Forres, near the mouth of the Findhorn. The distillery was built in 1898 and, despite refurbishment, seems to have been regarded as too old and small to keep alive. As a single malt, its whisky is available only from independent bottlers.

**House style** Big, flowery, traditional. After dinner.

---

### BENROMACH 1971, 40 vol, Connoisseurs Choice
**Colour** Amber.

---

**Nose** Big, sherryish, flowery.

---

**Body** Medium to full, creamy.

---

**Palate** Malty, sweet, rounded, but masked by sherry and oak.

---

**Finish** Sappy, oaky, slightly smoky.

---

### SCORE 77

**Other versions of Benromach**
Cadenhead has bottled 27- and 28-year-olds. The younger, with less sherry, revealed more of this malt's original floweriness but suffered from woodiness. SCORE 76. The older was well-balanced, but even a touch more woody. SCORE 76.

# BLADNOCH

**Producer** United Distillers
**Region** Lowlands   **District** Borders

THE MOST SOUTHERLY of Scotland's distilleries, and a definitive Lowland malt. The distillery stands far from any other, by a stone bridge across the Bladnoch River, near Wigtown, in Galloway, where the local accent sounds almost Northern Irish. The area is very rural, with a relatively mild climate. Bladnoch was founded between 1817 and 1825 as a farmhouse distillery, using barley grown on the hills behind. Its whisky has never been as widely appreciated as it deserves, and the distillery has been sold many times. It was mothballed in 1993.

**House style** Grassy, lemony, soft. Perhaps a dessert malt.

**BLADNOCH 8-year-old, 40 vol**
This light but distinctive version was bottled during Bell's ownership of the distillery. It can still be found on some shelves.

**Colour** Pale yellow.

**Nose** Grassy, lemony character right from the start.

**Body** Very light, but firm.

**Palate** At first seems delicate in flavour, but this develops and becomes surprisingly full.

**Finish** The citrus character emerges quite strongly in the finish, which is remarkably big for a light Lowland malt.

> SCORE 85

LOWLAND
SINGLE MALT
*SCOTCH WHISKY*

The *Broad Leaved Helleborine*,
a rare species of *wild orchid*, can be found growing
in the *ancient oak woodland* behind the

## BLADNOCH

*distillery.* The most southerly in *SCOTLAND*,
founded in the *early 1800's*, the
*distillery* stands by the *RIVER BLADNOCH*
near *Wigtown*. It produces a *distinctive*
*LOWLAND single MALT WHISKY – delicate* and
*fruity* with a *lemony aroma and taste.*

AGED **10** YEARS

43% vol    Distilled & Bottled in *SCOTLAND*.
BLADNOCH DISTILLERY, Bladnoch, Wigtownshire, Scotland    70 cl

### BLADNOCH 10-year-old, 43 vol, Flora and Fauna

**Colour** Amber.

**Nose** Hint of sherry, fragrantly fruity, lemony.

**Body** Fuller, firm.

**Palate** Lots of development, from a sherryish start through cereal-grain grassiness to flowery, fruity, lemony notes.

**Finish** Again, surprisingly big and long-lasting.

## SCORE 85

### BLADNOCH 1984, 40 vol, Connoisseurs Choice

**Colour** Deep gold.

**Nose** Honey and lemons.

**Body** Soft, luscious.

**Palate** Lemony, toffeeish.

**Finish** Smooth, with a touch of toffee.

## SCORE 86

### BLADNOCH 28-year-old, 42.5 vol, Cadenhead

**Colour** Darkish gold.

**Nose** Grassy, lemony.

**Body** Soft, rounded.

**Palate** Rounded, citric, malty, with some grassiness.

**Finish** Lemon, orange zest.

## SCORE 85

### Other versions of Bladnoch

For a light malt, Bladnoch ages very well. Even a 30-year-old, also from Cadenhead, had more distillery character than woodiness.

# BLAIR ATHOL

**Producer** United Distillers
**Region** Highlands **District** Midlands

 HE VILLAGE SPELLS ATHOLL with a double "l" while the distillery prefers to keep it single. Both are on the whisky route between Speyside and Perth. Pitlochry, known for its summer theatre, is not far away. The distillery traces its origins to 1798, and was extended in the 1970s.

**House style** Redolent of shortbread. A mid-afternoon malt?

---

### BLAIR ATHOL 8-year-old, 40 vol

**Colour** Pale gold.

**Nose** Fresh and very clean, with a suggestion of ginger or shortbread.

**Body** Light to medium.

**Palate** Dryish start. Aromatic. Hints of butterscotch and ginger.

**Finish** A little more gingery in its smooth, round finish.

SCORE 75

### BLAIR ATHOL 12-year-old, 43 vol

**Colour** Bronze.

**Nose** Still very fresh, some sherry, ginger shortbread.

**Body** Medium.

**Palate** Sherry, shortbread, ginger, fruity dryness.

**Finish** Smooth, round, warming.

SCORE 76

# BOWMORE

### Producer Morrison Bowmore
### Region Islay  District Loch Indaal

O NE OF THE GREAT malt distilleries, founded in 1779 in the village of Bowmore, "capital" of Islay. The village is in the middle of the island, on an inlet called Loch Indaal. In both geography and palate, the whiskies of Bowmore are between the intense malts of the south shore and the gentlest extremes of the north. Their character is not a compromise but an enigma, and tasters have found it difficult to unfold its complexity. The water used rises from iron-tinged rock, and picks up some peat from the earth as it flows by way of the River Laggan, through moss, ferns and rushes, to the distillery. While the peat higher on the island is rooty, that at Bowmore is sandier. The company has its own maltings, where the peat is crumbled before it is fired to give more smoke than heat. The malt is peated for a shorter time than that used for the more intense Islay whiskies. About 30 per cent of the whisky is aged in sherry. The distillery is more exposed to the westerly winds than others, so there may be more ozone in the complex of aromas and flavours.

**House style** Smoky, with leafy notes (ferns?) and sea-air.
Younger ages before dinner, older after.

*In this copper-domed mash tun, the barley malted at Bowmore and the island's peaty water meet and infuse on the way to becoming whisky.*

### BOWMORE 10-year-old, 40 vol

**Colour** Amber.

**Nose** Hint of sherry, light saltiness, spicy aromas, lavender, heather.

**Body** Light to medium.

**Palate** Lightly sweet, then spicy and heathery. Hint of smoke.

**Finish** Appetising. Lingering, late, saltiness. A delightful aperitif.

### SCORE 82

### BOWMORE 12-year-old, 43 vol

**Colour** Amber.

**Nose** More salt, seaweed and smoke than at 10 years.

**Body** Medium. Lightly syrupy.

**Palate** Persistent sherry sweetness. Spicy, heathery, seaweedy, salty. Complex, with lots of flavour development.

**Finish** Remarkably long and salty.

### SCORE 87

### BOWMORE Bicentenary (15-year-old, but no age statement), 43 vol

**Colour** Amber.

**Nose** Lots of flowering currant (a little too much for balance?).

**Body** Slightly oily.

**Palate** More sherry character. Heathery, seaweedy.

**Finish** Very long.

### SCORE 87

### BOWMORE 21-year-old (1972), 43 vol

**Colour** Full gold, with amber tinge.

**Nose** Hugely aromatic. Touch of sherry, hint of oak, plenty of smoke, very heathery and flowery, and robust seaweed and salt.

**Body** Medium to full, soft.

**Palate** Starts sweet, with notes of sherry and marzipan, developing to oiliness and salt. A remarkably complex, beautifully balanced whisky.

**Finish** Heathery, very aromatic, long and warming.

> **SCORE 90**

### BOWMORE 25-year-old (1968), 43 vol

**Colour** Full gold, with amber tinge.

**Nose** Fragrant balance of sherry sweetness, lavender leafiness and saltiness.

**Body** Medium to full, smooth.

**Palate** Sherry, some oak, marzipan, heather, lavender, seaweed and salt.

**Finish** Sherryish, smooth, then salty.

> **SCORE 89**

### BOWMORE 29-year-old, 49.4 vol, Cadenhead

**Colour** Pale gold.

**Nose** Dry, lightly phenolic.

**Body** Medium.

**Palate** Sweetish, leafy, developing towards herbal notes.

**Finish** Salty.

> **SCORE 80**

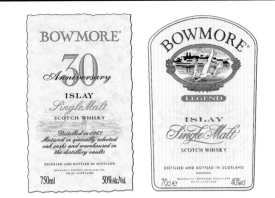

### BOWMORE 30-year-old, 50 vol
Subtitled "Anniversary" because it was distilled in the year that the Morrison family acquired the distillery.

**Colour** Deep greeny-gold.

**Nose** Some phenol, oily, dry.

**Body** Medium, soft.

**Palate** Sherryish, but less obviously so. Oily, earthy, very leafy, smoky.

**Finish** Smoky, herbal, long.

### SCORE 88

### BOWMORE LEGEND, no age statement, 40 vol
A light, young (five to eight years?) version, at a competitive price.

**Colour** Full gold.

**Nose** Peaty, smoky, very appetising.

**Body** Light but textured.

**Palate** Firm, a touch of iron, leafy, ferny, peaty. Earthy sweetness. Flavours very singular, and not yet melded. A fresh, young whisky, but no obvious spiritiness.

**Finish** Sweet, then salty.

### SCORE 80

### BLACK BOWMORE 1964, 50 vol
A rare and very unusual malt.

**Colour** Unusually dark. Reddish-brown, with black olive tinges.

**Nose** Lots of sherry. No excessive oakiness. Earthy, smoky, medicinal.

**Body** Medium, firm.

**Palate** Very sweet sherry notes, oaky, earthy, peaty. Astonishingly flowery for such a heavily sherried whisky. Sweetness and dryness. With a dash of water, endless complexities emerge.

**Finish** Cough linctus. Licorice. Very big and extremely long.

### SCORE 90

# BRACKLA

**Producer** United Distillers
**Region** Highlands   **District** Speyside (Findhorn Valley)

MAJESTIC MALT. The distillery lies between the River Findhorn and the Moray Firth at Cawdor, not far from Nairn. It was founded in 1812, and permitted to style itself "Royal Brackla" in 1835 because King William IV enjoyed the whisky. Royal Brackla was rebuilt in 1898 and again in 1966. It was extended in 1970. It closed in 1985 but was reopened in 1991. A Flora and Fauna bottling was released in 1993–94.

**House style** Fruity, burnt. After dinner.

---

**ROYAL BRACKLA 10-year-old, 43 vol, Flora and Fauna**

**Colour** Pale gold.

**Nose** Smoky, slightly sulphurous, burnt, molasses.

**Body** Medium, drying on the tongue.

**Palate** Starts malty and sweet, becoming robustly fruity (melon? raisins?) and moves towards spicy notes.

**Finish** Cedary, smoky.

**SCORE 74**

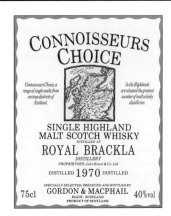

**ROYAL BRACKLA 1970, 40 vol, Connoisseurs Choice**
Despite its powerful sweetness, a perilously drinkable after-dinner malt. It also has a wonderful balance of peat smoke and malt, the classic ingredients.

**Colour** Old gold.

**Nose** Big, smoky aroma, with malty notes – almost a hint of molasses.

**Body** Medium to full.

**Palate** Extraordinarily smooth, malty and chewy. Develops an intense sweetness, becoming fruity (raisiny?) and perfumy.

**Finish** Very dry, with a cedary, cigar box character.

SCORE 77

**ROYAL BRACKLA 23-year-old, 46 vol, Cadenhead**

**Colour** Bright gold.

**Nose** Malty, sweetish, with some smokiness at the back of the nose.

**Body** Soft at first, becoming slightly dry on the tongue.

**Palate** Sweetish, perfumy.

**Finish** Dry, warming, very long.

SCORE 76

# BRAES OF GLENLIVET

**Producer** Seagram/Chivas
**Region** Highlands **District** Speyside (Livet)

**B**RAE IS A SCOTTISH-GAELIC word derived from Old Norse and meaning "a hillside" or "steep bank". Against a backdrop of a mountain ridge, this distillery is perched on a rocky, fast-flowing stream that feeds the River Livet. It is the highest distillery in the Livet district, in a remote spot just beyond the hamlet of Chapeltown, which is said to have been a refuge for religious dissidents in times of conflict. There was an earlier distillery with a similar name on a different site, but this one was built as recently (in whisky terms) as 1973–74, and expanded in 1975 and 1978. With latticed windows and a decorative pagoda, it looks as much like a place of worship as a distillery. Its whisky is intended as a component of the Chivas Regal blend and has yet to be bottled as a single malt, but it must surely emerge any moment from one of the independent merchants.

**House style** Light, sweet, honeyish. Aperitif.

### BRAES OF GLENLIVET 1979, cask strength

| | |
|---|---|
| **Colour** | Bright greeny-gold. |
| **Nose** | Light, honey and flowers. |
| **Body** | Light, soft, with a touch of viscosity. |
| **Palate** | Light, honeyish, emphatically sweet, clean, long. |
| **Finish** | Drying bite of orange peel, then lingering zest. |

### SCORE 74

*A modern distillery with architectural allusions to the past. Braes of Glenlivet is one of several distilleries built in the 1970s.*

# BRUICHLADDICH

**Producer** Invergordon
**Region** Islay   **District** Loch Indaal

GOOD SINGLE MALT for the newcomer to Islay. Bruichladdich is on the north shore of Loch Indaal, facing Bowmore across the water. Bruichladdich's water rises from a hillside spring, and flows over peat. It is, however, a less peaty water than some used by other distilleries. Its stills have tall necks, producing a relatively light, clean spirit. Unlike the other Islay distilleries, it is separated from the sea, albeit only by a quiet coast road. It was founded in 1881, rebuilt in 1886 and, despite an extension in 1975 remains little changed. Bruichladdich is now the most westerly working distillery in Scotland.

**House style** Light to medium, firm, salty. Very drinkable. Aperitif.

**BRUICHLADDICH 10-year-old, 40 vol**

| |
|---|
| **Colour** Pale gold. |
| **Nose** Very flowery, heathery, lightly seaweedy, emphatically salty. |
| **Body** Light to medium, smooth and firm. |
| **Palate** Firm and dry at first, with a touch of iron. Slight oiliness, and a suggestion of peat. Becoming maltier and sweeter, with touches of heather. Very slightly spirity. |
| **Finish** Long, with a range of subtle flavours. |

> SCORE 77

### BRUICHLADDICH 15-year-old, 40 vol

**Colour** Old gold.

**Nose** Intense. Drier, flowery, seaweedy, salty.

**Body** Firm, smooth, lightly oily.

**Palate** Flowery, seaweedy, salty. Flavours very well-combined and rounded. An easily drinkable yet satisfying malt. Has definitely benefited from the extra five years.

**Finish** Long, warming, salty.

SCORE 78

### BRUICHLADDICH 21-year-old, 43 vol

**Colour** Full gold.

**Nose** Intense, complex, appetising.

**Body** Medium, very firm.

**Palate** All the flavours intensify. Big maltiness in the middle, developing to powerful salt. For a relatively gentle whisky, a surprising lack of woodiness at this age.

**Finish** Complex, dry, salty, appetising.

SCORE 79

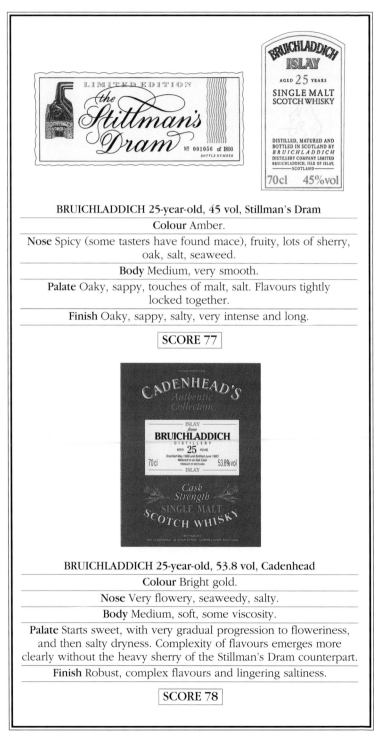

### BRUICHLADDICH 25-year-old, 45 vol, Stillman's Dram

**Colour** Amber.

**Nose** Spicy (some tasters have found mace), fruity, lots of sherry, oak, salt, seaweed.

**Body** Medium, very smooth.

**Palate** Oaky, sappy, touches of malt, salt. Flavours tightly locked together.

**Finish** Oaky, sappy, salty, very intense and long.

### SCORE 77

### BRUICHLADDICH 25-year-old, 53.8 vol, Cadenhead

**Colour** Bright gold.

**Nose** Very flowery, seaweedy, salty.

**Body** Medium, soft, some viscosity.

**Palate** Starts sweet, with very gradual progression to floweriness, and then salty dryness. Complexity of flavours emerges more clearly without the heavy sherry of the Stillman's Dram counterpart.

**Finish** Robust, complex flavours and lingering saltiness.

### SCORE 78

# BUNNAHABHAIN

**Producer** Highland Distilleries
**Region** Islay   **District** North shore

**A**LTHOUGH BUNNAHABHAIN IS sometimes described as the Islay malt that lacks the island character, that is to misunderstand this delicious whisky. Among the Islay malts, it is the lightest in palate, but its body has a distinctive oiliness. It has a faint, flowery, nutty hint of peatiness, a whiff of sea air, and a character that is quietly distinctive. The distillery, established in 1881, is set around a courtyard in a style reminiscent of a château in Bordeaux. Despite expansion in 1963, the distillery has changed little. Its water is piped from streams in the hills, and is therefore less peaty than might be expected. The stills are large, in a style that the industry refers to as onion-shaped, although pear-shaped might be a better description. Bunnahabhain emphasises the narrowness of the cut taken from the stills. A small proportion of sherry is used in maturation. A 1964 vintage from Signatory is more intense, and maltier than the official version.

**House style** Fresh, nutty. Aperitif.

---

**BUNNAHABHAIN 12-year-old, 40 vol**

**Colour** Gold.

**Nose** Remarkably fresh sea-air aroma.

**Body** Light to medium, firm.

**Palate** Gentle, clean, nutty-malty sweetness.

**Finish** Very full flavour development. A refreshing quality.

SCORE 77

# CAOL ILA

**Producer** United Distillers
**Region** Islay   **District** North shore

L ONG-ENJOYED BY DEVOTEES as a very distinctive malt, with a lot of attack for its side of the island. The name, pronounced "cull-eela", means "Sound of Islay". The Gaelic word "caol" is more familiar as "kyle". The distillery is in a cove near Port Askaig, overlooking the Sound of Islay, across which the ferry chugs to the nearby island of Jura. A peaty loch about a mile away sends water across fields to Caol Ila, which has large, lantern-shaped stills. The distillery was built in 1846, reconstructed in 1879, and brusquely modernised in the 1970s. Its whisky has been a component of a vatted malt, called Glen Ila, and the Bulloch Lade blends, which are traditionally popular in several export markets. A Bulloch Lade bottling may be found, as well as a Flora and Fauna version. Judging from the independent bottlings, this malt has very rarely been aged in sherry, and it is a good example of a whisky that seems not to need that refinement.

**House style** Oily, olive-like. A wonderful aperitif.

| CAOL ILA 12-year-old, 40 vol, Bulloch Lade |
|---|
| **Colour** Pale, white wine. |
| **Nose** Peaty, seaweedy, fruity. |
| **Body** Light, but very firm, becoming slightly syrupy. |
| **Palate** Peaty, peppery, spicy, olive-like. |
| **Finish** Peppery, warming. |

SCORE 77

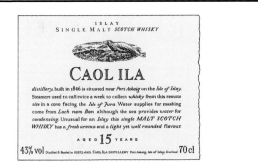

ISLAY
SINGLE MALT *SCOTCH WHISKY*

## CAOL ILA

*distillery,* built in 1846 is situated near *Port Askaig* on the *Isle of Islay.*
Steamers used to call twice a week to collect *whisky* from this remote
*site* in a cove facing the *Isle of Jura.* Water supplies for mashing
come from *Loch nam Ban* although the sea provides *water* for
*condensing.* Unusual for an *Islay* this *single MALT SCOTCH
WHISKY* has a *fresh* aroma and a *light* yet *well rounded* flavour.

AGED **15** YEARS

43% vol   Distilled & Bottled in SCOTLAND. CAOL ILA DISTILLERY Port Askaig, Isle of Islay, Scotland. 70 cl

### CAOL ILA 15-year-old, 43 vol, Flora and Fauna

**Colour** Fino sherry, bright.

**Nose** Aromatic, complex.

**Body** Light, very firm, smooth.

**Palate** Rounder, with the flavours more combined.

**Finish** Oily and warming enough to keep out the sea.

### SCORE 80

### CAOL ILA 1980, 40 vol, Connoisseurs Choice

**Colour** Gold, with amber tinge.

**Nose** Fresh sea air.

**Body** Surprisingly light, smooth.

**Palate** Seaweedy, oily, like sucking on a green olive.
Touch of sherry.

**Finish** Very salty (reminiscent of anchovies), hugely expressive.

### SCORE 78

### Other versions of Caol Ila

From Cadenhead, a 16-year-old at 60.2 vol had more intensity on
the nose, pepperiness and bitterness. SCORE 79. A 1978 at cask
strength from Oddbins was dry, oily and very salty. SCORE 78. An
18-year-old (1974) at 61.1 vol from Signatory was very peppery,
toasty and perhaps a touch woody. SCORE 77.

# CAPERDONICH

**Producer** Seagram/Chivas
**Region** Highlands **District** Speyside (Rothes)

**P**ARTNER TO THE RENOWNED Glen Grant. The two distilleries, under the same ownership, are across the street from one another in the whisky town of Rothes. This little town on the Spey has five distilleries. Caperdonich, founded in 1898, was rebuilt in 1965 and extended in 1967. From the start, it has been number two to Glen Grant. The malts of both distilleries are light and fragrant in their bouquet, medium-bodied and nutty-tasting. Of the two, Caperdonich is perhaps a dash fruitier and slightly more smoky. They are also components of the Chivas Regal blend. As a single, Caperdonich is available only in independent bottlings, although this may change.

**House style** Fruity, creamy. After dinner.

**CAPERDONICH 1968, 40 vol, Connoisseurs Choice**
The lesser-known Speyside malts can still have plenty of style, and this is a good example.

| | |
|---|---|
| **Colour** Full, golden. | |
| **Nose** Fragrant, smoky. | |
| **Body** Light to medium, dryish. | |
| **Palate** Malty, nutty and fruity. A hint of coconut? | |
| **Finish** Seems at first abrupt, but turns out to be lingering, warming and slightly smoky. | |

**SCORE 73**

## CAPERDONICH 14-year-old, 60.5 vol, Cadenhead

**Colour** Gold, with reddish tinge.

**Nose** Hessian. Stringy, leafy notes. Earth.

**Body** Soft, syrupy.

**Palate** Syrupy, fruity, spicy, dryish. Coconut? Cloves?

**Finish** Dry, fruity, spicy, aromatic.

SCORE 75

# CARDHU

**Producer** United Distillers
**Region** Highlands   **District** Speyside

LTHOUGH IT EXISTED illicitly before its official establishment in 1824, this distillery was rebuilt in 1872 by Elizabeth Cumming, the founder's daughter-in-law, who is still remembered as one of the great figures of the industry. Her son became a director of Johnnie Walker, and at least one of her descendants is still in the whisky business. The slightly syrupy, sweetish whisky of Cardhu has always been the soft heart of the Johnnie Walker blends (in which it is balanced by the feistily evident Talisker, among many others). In recent years, it has been widely marketed as a single malt. Independent bottlings can occasionally be found, sometimes using older spellings of the name. Cardhu is on a hillside near the Spey, in the heart of malt-whisky country.

**House style** Light, smooth, sweetish, delicate.
An easy-drinking malt.

---

### CARDHU 12-year-old, 40 vol

**Colour** Pale.

**Nose** Light, appetising, with a faint hint of smoke.

**Body** Light and smooth.

**Palate** Light to medium in flavour, with the emphasis on malty sweetness.

**Finish** A lingering, syrupy sweetness, but also a rounder dryness with late hints of peat, although again faint.

SCORE 72

# CLYNELISH

**Producer** United Distillers
**Region** Highlands    **District** North Highlands

**A** CLASSIC CASE of a coastal malt having a slightly "island" character. The location is the fishing and golfing resort of Brora, which gave its name to a distillery established in 1819. Across the road and founded in 1967 is the present Clynelish distillery. For much of its history, the older distillery used highly peated malt. Clynelish uses a medium peating. The malt from the older distillery may still appear from independent bottlers or retail chains.

**House style** Seaweedy, spicy. With a roast-beef sandwich.

**CLYNELISH 14-year-old, 43 vol, Flora and Fauna**

**Colour** Pale gold.

**Nose** Sea, perhaps seaweed, and peat.

**Body** Medium to full, smooth. Visibly oily.

**Palate** Starts malty (sweetish when water is added), becoming fruity-spicy (mustard?), with notes of seaweed and salt.

**Finish** Remarkable lingering spiciness. Stays very fresh, with an emphatic mustard flavour. Reminiscent of mustard-cress. A tremendously appetising malt.

**SCORE 81**

## BRORA 1972, 40 vol, Connoisseurs Choice

**Colour** Full gold to bronze.

**Nose** Iodine, seaweed, salt.

**Body** Medium to full, firm, oily.

**Palate** Seaweedy, but less than the nose would suggest. Dry, salty. After the pungency of the aroma, a relatively delicate palate.

**Finish** Light, dry, salty.

### SCORE 81

## CLYNELISH 28-year-old (1965), 50.7 vol, Signatory

**Colour** Bronze.

**Nose** Fresh, seaweedy.

**Body** Medium to full, smooth, oily.

**Palate** Hint of sherry, smooth, sweetish, mustardy, seaweedy. Well-balanced.

**Finish** Smooth, touch of sweetness, late salt.

### SCORE 82

**Other versions of Clynelish**

An 11-year-old at 66.7 vol from Cadenhead was very distinctive, with a very long and spicy, very mustardy and warming finish. SCORE 82. A full-bodied 12-year-old at 57 vol from Gordon and MacPhail had a salty, spicy nose with a touch of sherry, and an extraordinarily long and complex finish. SCORE 82. A 1972 bottling at cask strength from Oddbins was deep amber in colour, with an oaky, mustardy, dry finish. SCORE 80.

# AN CNOC

**Producer** Knockdhu Distillery Company
**Region** Highlands   **District** Speyside

**T**O AVOID CONFUSION with Knockando, this malt changed its name from Knockdhu to An Cnoc. Either way, the name refers to its location at the village of Knock, between the Rivers Isla and Deveron. The name of the whisky and the village refer to a nearby "dark hill". The distillery was built in 1894 to supply malt for the Haig blends, closed in 1983, then acquired and reopened by the partners of Inver House, a firm of blenders. The first official bottling of a single malt came in 1990, initially under the older name.

**House style** Creamy and fruity. A dessert malt?

| AN CNOC 12-year-old, 40 vol |
| :--- |
| **Colour** Pale gold. |
| **Nose** Very aromatic, smooth, fruity. Pineapple? |
| **Body** Light but very smooth. |
| **Palate** Smooth, creamy, vanilla notes. Very soft note of fruit. Very drinkable and enjoyable. |
| **Finish** Creamy, oaty. Sweet herbs. |

### SCORE 75

**Other versions of Knockdhu**
A 1974 bottled under the older name (Connoisseurs Choice) had a hint of smoke, more creaminess and maltiness, a touch of sherry and a longer finish. SCORE 75.

# COLEBURN

**Producer** United Distillers
**Region** Highlands   **District** Speyside (Lossie)

CONNOISSEURS CHOICE

*Connoisseurs Choice, a range of single malts from various districts of Scotland.*

*The distilleries situated in the area of the valley of the River Spey produce some of the finest malt whiskies.*

GRAMPIANS

SINGLE SPEYSIDE
MALT SCOTCH WHISKY
*DISTILLED AT*

COLEBURN
DISTILLERY
PROPRIETORS: J. & G. Stewart Ltd

DISTILLED 1972 DISTILLED

*SPECIALLY SELECTED, PRODUCED AND BOTTLED BY*
75cl   GORDON & MACPHAIL   40%vol
ELGIN · SCOTLAND
PRODUCT OF SCOTLAND

T HE PIONEERING BLENDER Andrew Usher created the brands that came to use the Coleburn distillery. Its malt whisky was also used in the Johnnie Walker blends. The distillery, on the east of the River Lossie, was built in 1896. A small, old-fashioned distillery, it was temporarily closed in 1985 and seems unlikely to reopen.

**House style** Dry, lively. Aperitif.

---

**COLEBURN 1972, 40 vol, Connoisseurs Choice**

---

**Colour** Fuller gold.

---

**Nose** Sweetness and dryness, with a hint of smoke.

---

**Body** Light but firm.

---

**Palate** Slightly oily, cereal-grain, sweetness. Becoming drier and faintly smoky.

---

**Finish** Still oily-sweet, becoming dry, warming. Falls away somewhat.

---

SCORE 66

### Other versions of Coleburn

A 1965 Connoisseurs Choice had a bigger, more flowery bouquet and a raisiny sweetness. SCORE 67. A 1979 (bottled 1988), from the Scotch Malt Whisky Society, had more fruit and sherry, and was remarkably lively. SCORE 69. Neither has been bottled for some time, but they may be found on the odd shelf.

# CONVALMORE

**Producer** William Grant and Sons
**Region** Highlands   **District** Speyside (Dufftown)

**C**HEEK-BY-JOWL with Glenfiddich and Balvenie, and under the same ownership since 1992, Convalmore may have been secured as a component for the Grant's blend. The distillery was founded in 1894, and mothballed in 1985.

**House style** Malty, syrupy, fruity, biggish. After dinner.

### CONVALMORE 1969, 40 vol, Connoisseurs Choice
An unassuming, enjoyable digestif.

**Colour** Full gold.

**Nose** Very pleasant, sweetish.

**Body** Medium to full.

**Palate** Smooth, slightly syrupy texture. At first sweet, but not at all cloying. Develops towards malty dryness.

**Finish** Hints of ginger, spiciness and peat in an aromatic, dry finish.

SCORE 68

### CONVALMORE 30-year-old, 46.5 vol, Cadenhead

**Colour** Gold.

**Nose** Honeyish, touch of peat.

**Body** Medium to full.

**Palate** Malty, soft fruitiness (pears in syrup?). Surprising lack of woodiness.

**Finish** Smooth, long, spicy, heathery, touch of peat.

SCORE 75

# CRAGGANMORE

**Producer** United Distillers
**Region** Highlands   **District** Speyside

ONE OF THE GREAT Speyside malts, but less widely known than might be expected. This is a whisky for the connoisseur, from a relatively small distillery, although it is promoted in United Distillers' "Classic Malts" range. Cragganmore is a respected distillery, founded in 1869 and boasting an interesting history. It is very pretty, hidden in a hollow high on the Spey. Its water, from nearby springs, is relatively hard, and its spirit stills have an unusual, flat-topped shape. These two elements may be factors in the complexity of the malt, which is matured in re-fill sherry casks. The malt is used in the Macallum blends, which are popular in Australasia.

**House style** Austere, stonily dry, aromatic. After dinner.

### CRAGGANMORE 12-year-old, 40 vol

**Colour** Golden.

**Nose** The most complex aroma of any malt. Its bouquet is astonishingly fragrant and delicate, with sweetish notes of cut grass and herbs (thyme perhaps?).

**Body** Light to medium, but very firm and smooth.

**Palate** Delicate, clean, restrained, with a huge range of herbal flowery notes.

**Finish** Long.

### SCORE 90

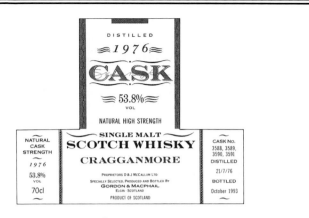

**CRAGGANMORE 1976, 53.8 vol, Gordon and MacPhail**

**Colour** Pale gold.

**Nose** Fragrant, lightly peaty, grassy, nutty, herbal.

**Body** Medium, very smooth.

**Palate** Complex, restrained, with rooty, licorice notes.

**Finish** Long, more licorice, enveloping.

SCORE 89

**CRAGGANMORE 1974, 40 vol, Connoisseurs Choice**

**Colour** Slightly fuller than the 1972 version.

**Nose** Slightly softer. Fragrant, with light peat-smoke.

**Body** Full but soft.

**Palate** Astonishingly perfumy and spicy. More complex.

**Finish** Gentler, but very long.

SCORE 88

# CRAIGELLACHIE

**Producer** United Distillers
**Region** Highlands  **District** Speyside

W HERE THE FIDDICH meets the Spey, and the district's main roads cross – between Dufftown, Aberlour and Rothes – the village of Craigellachie has a bridge, designed by the great Scottish engineer Thomas Telford, a cooperage, and two distilleries. The one called simply Craigellachie stands to the southeast of the Spey, northwest is Macallan. Craigellachie is pronounced "Craig-ella-ki" – the "i" is short. Its full-flavoured, malty-fruity whisky is a component of the White Horse blends. As a single malt, it is available in the Flora and Fauna series bottled by United Distillers. The distillery was founded in 1891 and rebuilt in 1965.

**House style** Sweet, nutty, fruity. After dinner.

SPEYSIDE
SINGLE MALT
*SCOTCH WHISKY*

CRAIGELLACHIE

*distillery,* founded in 1888, in the *county of*
BANFFSHIRE. *stands overlooking the*
RIVER SPEY, the rock of *Craigellachie,* and
TELFORD'S single span iron BRIDGE. The
distillery uses local *spring water* running from
little CONVAL HILL for *mashing, resulting*
in this excellent *single* MALT SCOTCH
WHISKY of light and *smoky character.*

AGED 14 YEARS

43% vol        70cl

---

**CRAIGELLACHIE 14-year-old, 43 vol, Flora and Fauna**

**Colour** Old gold.

**Nose** Fragrant. Lightly smoky. Plenty of sweet, crushed-barley maltiness.

**Body** Medium.

**Palate** Starts sweet, slightly syrupy and malty, then becomes nutty, developing a very fruity, Seville orange character.

**Finish** Orangey, lightly smoky, aromatic, warming.

**SCORE 75**

### CRAIGELLACHIE 1974, 40 vol, Gordon and MacPhail

**Colour** Amber.

**Nose** More emphatic and complex in its fragrance.

**Body** Medium.

**Palate** Softer. Nutty. Falls away somewhat.

**Finish** Lightly smoky, gently warming.

SCORE 73

### CRAIGELLACHIE 26-year-old, 46 vol, Cadenhead

**Colour** Pale, white wine.

**Nose** Fragrant, dry.

**Body** Very soft and smooth.

**Palate** Minty and malty, sweetish. Distinctive and enjoyable.

**Finish** Minty, rather quick.

SCORE 72

# DAILUAINE

**Producer** United Distillers
**Region** Highlands **District** Speyside

**B**ETWEEN THE MOUNTAIN Ben Rinnes and the River Spey, at the hamlet of Carron, not far from Aberlour, the Dailuaine ("Dal-oo-ayn") distillery is hidden in a hollow. The name means green vale, and that accurately describes the setting. It was founded in 1852 and has been rebuilt several times since. It is one of several distilleries along the Spey valley that once had its own railway halts, for workers and visitors – and as a means of shipping in barley or malt and despatching the whisky. Although most of the line is long gone, the route of the track has been preserved for walkers as the Speyside Way, leading from Tomintoul to the sea. It even had its own steam locomotive, now preserved on a surviving stretch of the Strathspey Railway at Aviemore. Dailuaine's whisky has long been a component of the Johnnie Walker blends, and has been available as a single malt in the Flora and Fauna series since 1991.

**House style** Malty, fruity, perfumy. After dinner.

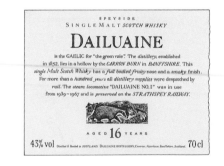

SPEYSIDE
SINGLE MALT *SCOTCH WHISKY*

## DAILUAINE

is the GAELIC for "the green vale". The *distillery*, established in 1852, lies in a hollow by the *CARRON BURN* in *BANFFSHIRE*. This *single Malt Scotch Whisky* has a *full bodied fruity* nose and a *smoky* finish. For more than a *hundred years* all *distillery supplies* were despatched by rail. The *steam locomotive* "DAILUAINE NO.1" was in use from 1939 – 1967 and is *preserved* on the *STRATHSPEY RAILWAY*.

AGED **16** YEARS

43% vol Distilled & Bottled in SCOTLAND. DAILUAINE DISTILLERY, Carron, Aberlour, Banffshire, Scotland. 70 cl

**DAILUAINE 16-year-old, 43 vol, Flora and Fauna**

| | |
|---|---|
| **Colour** | Emphatically reddish-amber. |
| **Nose** | Sherryish but dry, perfumy. |
| **Body** | Medium to full, smooth. |
| **Palate** | Sherryish, with barley-sugar maltiness, but balanced by a dry cedar or oak background. |
| **Finish** | Sherryish, smooth, very warming, long. |

**SCORE 76**

## DAILUAINE 1971, 40 vol, Connoisseurs Choice

**Colour** Gold.

**Nose** Fragrant, long-lasting, beginning dry, with malty notes and a suggestion of sherry, gradually becoming sweeter.

**Body** Medium to full, quite fleshy.

**Palate** Restrained sweetness, some syrupy maltiness and a dash of fruit.

**Finish** Oaky.

### SCORE 74

**DAILUAINE 22-year-old, 46 vol, Cadenhead**

**Colour** Very pale, white wine.

**Nose** Fragrant, on the dry side, but with some sweet notes.

**Body** Medium to full, soft.

**Palate** Sweet, fruity, aromatic.

**Finish** Soft, fruity, aromatic. A 23-year-old version is perhaps marginally drier.

### SCORE 73

**Other versions of Dailuaine**

A Scotch Malt Whisky Society bottling 1975 at 57.3 vol had a greenish hue, a smokier nose, but a sweeter palate. Not so much barley sugar as toffee. SCORE 72. A 13-year-old (1978) at 64.8 vol from the Society had a similar colour, a drily heather-honey nose and a dry but sherryish palate. SCORE 73.

# DALLAS DHU

**Producer** United Distillers
**Region** Highlands    **District** Speyside (Findhorn)

**P**RESERVED FOR POSTERITY, but no longer producing its delicious, rich malt. Founded in 1899, and little changed since, it closed in the early 1980s and reopened to the public in 1988, under the aegis of Scotland's Historic Buildings and Monument Directorate. There are no plans to restart production, but the later batches continue to appear in independent bottlings.

**House style** Very rich flavours. After dinner.

| DALLAS DHU 10-year-old, 40 vol, Gordon and MacPhail |
|---|
| **Colour** Amber. |
| **Nose** Peaty, malty, sherryish, complex. |
| **Body** Medium, very smooth. |
| **Palate** Malt, dark chocolate. |
| **Finish** Smooth, chocolatey. |

### SCORE 80

**Other versions of Dallas Dhu**

A Signatory 1974 at 60.8 vol was a bright gold in colour, more flowery on the nose, fuller in body and more honeyed in palate. SCORE 80. A Connoisseurs Choice 1971 at 40 vol was complex, with some sappy oakiness and a very long finish. SCORE 85. A Cadenhead 30-year-old at 53.3 vol was a fuller gold in colour, slightly woody on the nose, full in palate, with concentrated honey flavours and a flowery finish. SCORE 80.

# THE DALMORE

**Producer** Whyte and Mackay
**Region** Highlands  **District** Northern Highlands

O NCE OWNED BY a distinguished local family, the Mackenzies, friends of James Whyte and Charles Mackay who created a famous name in blended Scotch. The Dalmore distillery, said to have been founded in 1839, bears a passing resemblance to a country railway station. Its offices are panelled with carved oak that once graced a shooting lodge. The soft, full-bodied water comes from the River Alness, which flows through forest. The wash stills have an unusually conical upper chamber and the spirit stills are cooled with a water jacket – another distinctive feature. There are two pairs of stills, identical in shape but different sizes. The warehouses are by the waters of the Cromarty Firth. About 85 per cent of the whisky is matured in Bourbon casks, mainly first-fill, the rest in sweet oloroso and amontillado, but it is all married in sherry butts. Some blenders compare Dalmore whisky to the Merlot claret. It seems to attract other flavours, harmonising them and providing a certain lushness.

**House style** Rich, flavourful, orange marmalade. After dinner.

| DALMORE 12-year-old, 40 vol |
| --- |
| **Colour** Full amber. |
| **Nose** Powerful, with fruit (orange marmalade?), malt and sherry. |
| **Body** Medium to full. Velvet-smooth. |
| **Palate** Rich, with gradual restrained flavour development. Malty sweetness, bittersweet orange, spiciness (anise?), perfuminess, heather, light peat; even a faint, salty tang of the sea. |
| **Finish** Remarkably long. |

SCORE 79

### DALMORE 18-year-old, 54.8 vol, Cullicudden

**Colour** Gold.

**Nose** Light heather and fruit.

**Body** Medium and syrupy.

**Palate** Very malty, light fruit, touches of heather and salt.

**Finish** Syrupy, lightly heathery, very salty.

**SCORE 75**

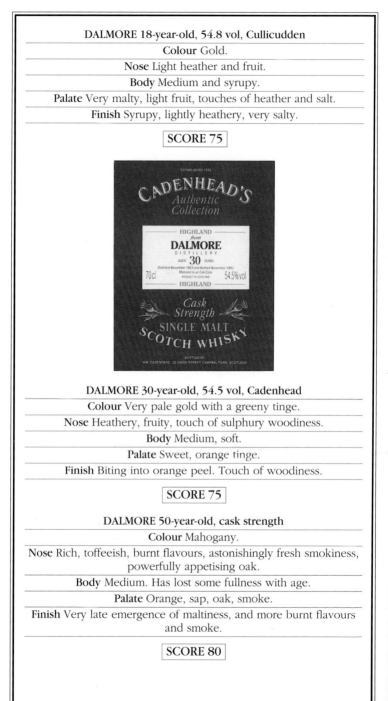

### DALMORE 30-year-old, 54.5 vol, Cadenhead

**Colour** Very pale gold with a greeny tinge.

**Nose** Heathery, fruity, touch of sulphury woodiness.

**Body** Medium, soft.

**Palate** Sweet, orange tinge.

**Finish** Biting into orange peel. Touch of woodiness.

**SCORE 75**

### DALMORE 50-year-old, cask strength

**Colour** Mahogany.

**Nose** Rich, toffeeish, burnt flavours, astonishingly fresh smokiness, powerfully appetising oak.

**Body** Medium. Has lost some fullness with age.

**Palate** Orange, sap, oak, smoke.

**Finish** Very late emergence of maltiness, and more burnt flavours and smoke.

**SCORE 80**

# DALWHINNIE

**Producer** United Distillers
**Region** Highlands   **District** Speyside

**T**HE HIGHEST DISTILLERY in Scotland, at 326m (1,073ft), Dalwhinnie lies in a glen, with the Monadhlaith Mountains to one side, and the Forest of Atholl, the Cairngorms and the Grampians to the other. Its name is Gaelic for "meeting place". The village of the same name stands at the junction of old cattle-droving routes from the west and north down to the central Lowlands. Much whisky smuggling went on along this route. The distillery was called Strathspey when it opened in 1897. Stretching a point, it can regard itself as being on Speyside, although it is 25 miles or more from the dense distillery country to the north. Its malt whisky has traditionally been an important component of the Buchanan blends, and it represents the Highlands in United Distillers' "Classic Malts" range.

**House style** Lightly peaty. Aperitif.

| DALWHINNIE 15-year-old, 43 vol |
|---|
| **Colour** Gold. |
| **Nose** Very aromatic, dry, faintly phenolic, lightly peaty. |
| **Body** Firm, slightly oily. |
| **Palate** Remarkably smooth, long-lasting flavour development. Aromatic, heather-honey notes give way to cut-grass, malty sweetness, which intensifies to a sudden burst of peat. |
| **Finish** Very long. |

### SCORE 76

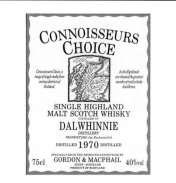

## DALWHINNIE 1970, 40 vol, Connoisseurs Choice

**Colour** Slightly fuller.

**Nose** More phenol, more emphatic peatiness.

**Body** Fuller, with some syrupiness.

**Palate** Less subtlety, but more Highland character.

**Finish** More emphatic.

SCORE 76

## DALWHINNIE 27-year-old, 45.5 vol, Cadenhead

**Colour** Full gold.

**Nose** Some grassy sweetness. Light peatiness.

**Body** Medium to full, syrupy.

**Palate** Some sweet maltiness, then grassy dryness.

**Finish** Assertive and somewhat peaty.

SCORE 76

### Other versions of Dalwhinnie

A 17-year-old (1975 bottling) at 57.8 vol from the Scotch Malt
Whisky Society was robust in flavours, with both a sweet, syrupy
maltiness and rough grassiness towards its long finish. SCORE 76.

# DEANSTON

**Producer** Burn Stewart
**Region** Highlands **District** Midlands

**T**HIS DISTILLERY IS IN the Highlands, but only by a few miles – it is at Doune, southwest of Perth. The town boasts a medieval castle and a former cotton mill designed by Richard Arkwright. The mill was originally water-driven and lies on the River Teith. The supply of good water apparently contributed to the decision to turn the mill into a distillery at a time when the whisky industry was doing very well. It opened as the Deanston distillery in 1965–66, with the vaulted weaving shed serving as a warehouse. The distillery prospered during the 1970s, but closed during the difficult mid-1980s. At the time it was owned by Invergordon. With the revival of the industry in the late 1980s and early 1990s, Deanston was bought by the blenders Burn Stewart, and more versions of this pleasant malt are now becoming available. A 1977 sample at 55 vol from the Scotch Malt Whisky Society was promisingly rich in its toffeeish maltiness.

**House style** Light, slightly oily, nutty. Restorative.

### DEANSTON 12-year-old, 40 vol

**Colour** Very pale, greeny-gold. Fino sherry.

**Nose** Linseed oil.

**Body** Light, smooth, soothing.

**Palate** Light, very clean. Lightly malty, drying in finish. Also reminiscent of a lightly nutty, dry sherry.

**Finish** Again, very light, but a touch of nuttiness. In character, less of a Highland malt than a very good Lowlander.

SCORE 70

**DEANSTON 16-year-old, 55 vol, Cadenhead**

**Colour** Very pale greenish-gold.

**Nose** Grassy.

**Body** Light, firmer.

**Palate** Sweetish start, toffeeish, nutty, becoming grassy, with bittersweet notes.

**Finish** Dry, herbal.

SCORE 71

**DEANSTON 17-year old, 40 vol**

**Colour** Markedly fuller. Bright bronze.

**Nose** Linseed oil, grass, cereal grain, barley sugar.

**Body** Light to medium.

**Palate** Cereal grain, more emphatically nutty. Slightly creamy.

**Finish** Nutty, appetising.

SCORE 71

**DEANSTON 25-year-old, 40 vol**

**Colour** Bronze.

**Nose** Cereal grain, nutty.

**Body** Medium, very smooth.

**Palate** Cereal grain, nutty, some sweetness.

**Finish** Touch of creaminess.

SCORE 71

# DRUMGUISH

**Producer** Speyside Distillery Company
**Region** Highlands   **District** Speyside

W HERE THE RIVER TROMIE flows into the Spey, a distillery was built in 1895. It was called Speyside and was dismantled before the First World War. Between the 1950s and the 1970s, a whisky blender, George Christie, conceived an ambition to build a new Speyside Distillery. He created a blend called Speyside and a vatted malt, Glentromie. His project for a single malt bubbled along for decades, ebbing and flowing according to the tides of the whisky industry and economy. The stone-built distillery finally opened in 1993. The single malt, called Drumguish after its precise location, is well aware of its tender years, and has no pretentions to being a wise old man of the mountains. The view was that if great malts offer themselves at five years in some markets, why shouldn't a newcomer take advantage of this? There will be a more mature malt in due course.

**House style** Dry, slightly oily, with a touch of peat. Aperitif.

---

DRUMGUISH 3-year-old, 40 vol

**Colour** Full gold.

**Nose** Flowery, dry, lightly peaty.

**Body** Light to medium, soft, drying on the tongue.

**Palate** Clean start, with a very brief creamy sweetness, quickly moving to a light oiliness and lightly peaty dryness. No excessive spiritiness.

**Finish** Lightly peaty, dry, with a very late touch of light fruitiness.

SCORE 70

*The buildings recall the 1890s, but the distillery is scarcely older than the whisky.*

# DUFFTOWN

**Producer** United Distillers
**Region** Highlands **District** Speyside (Dufftown)

T HE EARL OF FIFE, James Duff, laid out this town, which eponymously took his name. It lies at the confluence of the Rivers Fiddich and Dullan on their way to the Spey, and is pronounced "Duff-ton". There are seven malt distilleries in the town, of which only one appropriates Dufftown as its name. This distillery and Pittyvaich, its next-door neighbour, were both owned by Bells until that company was acquired by United Distillers. Dufftown's stone-built premises were a meal mill until 1896, but they have since sprouted a pagoda, and were twice expanded in the 1970s. Dufftown's malt is a good, no-nonsense Highland whisky.

**House style** Aromatic, dry, malty. Aperitif.

### DUFFTOWN 8-year-old, 40 vol

**Colour** Full, golden.

**Nose** Lightly aromatic, with hints of smoke and plenty of malty dryness.

**Body** Medium, rounded, firm and dryish.

**Palate** Seems to promise more than it delivers. Again, suggestions of smoke and a lot of malty dryness.

**Finish** A lingering viscosity on the tongue, but not a great deal of flavour.

| SCORE 70 |
|----------|

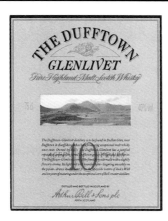

## DUFFTOWN 10-year-old, 40 vol

**Colour** Full, golden.

**Nose** A little more of everything. Very well-rounded.

**Body** Much more viscosity.

**Palate** Quite syrupy.

**Finish** Lacks flavour development.

SCORE 71

## DUFFTOWN 15-year-old, 43 vol, Flora and Fauna

**Colour** Pale golden.

**Nose** Assertively aromatic.

**Body** Lightly syrupy.

**Palate** Malty, on the dry side, becoming flowery.

**Finish** Lingers, but very light.

SCORE 71

# EDRADOUR

**Producer** Pernod/Campbell Distillers
**Region** Highlands **District** Midlands

T HE SMALLEST DISTILLERY in Scotland. Edradour is the last of the original farm distilleries, with some very traditional equipment. It likes to trace its history back to the beginning of legal whisky production in the Highlands in 1825, although the present distillery is believed to have been founded in 1837. The distillery is at the hamlet of Balnauld, above the town of Pitlochry. Small and remote, it is reputed to have done a busy trade with American customers during the Prohibition. One story maintains that it was later indirectly owned for a lengthy period by the Mafia, but this has not been substantiated. It produces as much malt whisky in a year as some distilleries can make in a week, and has a staff of three. Its water rises through peat and granite, reaching the surface a few hundred yards from the building. It uses local barley and its stills are the smallest in Scotland, which must contribute to the distinctive richness of the malt. Stills any smaller would not be permitted by Customs and Excise, for fear that they could be operated in a secret hiding place. In the late 1980s, Edradour began to bottle its whisky as a 10-year-old single malt under its own label.

**House style** Minty, creamy. After dinner.

*This classically pretty distillery is hidden in a glen. The approaching visitor crests a hill, and suddenly there it is in the hollow below.*

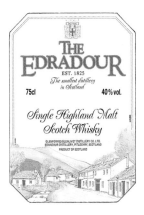

### EDRADOUR 10-year-old, 40 vol

**Colour** Full golden.

**Nose** Peppermint, sugared almonds, hint of sherry, spicy-smoky notes.

**Body** Remarkably creamy texture for a relatively light malt.

**Palate** Minty-clean, creamy, malty.

**Finish** Mellow, warming.

### SCORE 81

### EDRADOUR 1973, 40 vol, Gordon and MacPhail

**Colour** Bronze.

**Nose** More sherry character.

**Body** Light, but smooth and rounded.

**Palate** More nutty maltiness. Astonishingly creamy.

**Finish** Warming, enveloping, long.

### SCORE 85

### EDRADOUR 1968, 46 vol, Signatory

**Colour** Golden.

**Nose** Perfumy, dry.

**Body** Light but firm, oily.

**Palate** Very nutty (walnuts?), flowery, dry.

**Finish** Dry and rather abrupt.

### SCORE 80

# FETTERCAIRN

**Producer** Whyte and Mackay
**Region** Highlands **District** Eastern Highlands

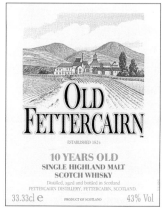

**B**ETWEEN THE CAIRNGORMS and the sea, the peaks, forests and glens hide a number of distilleries. The village and distillery of Fettercairn are near the glen of the North Esk, a river that flows into the sea not far from Montrose. Fettercairn is one of Scotland's oldest distilleries, reputed to have been founded in 1824. It was rebuilt several times around the turn of the century, and extended in 1966. The single malt is subtle, and easy to underrate. It was launched as an 8-year-old, then promoted to a 10-year-old. A dash of sherry, a couple more years, and perhaps a marginally higher alcohol content do make a difference.

**House style** Lightly earthy, nutty. Easy drinking or aperitif.

### OLD FETTERCAIRN 10-year-old, 43 vol

**Colour** Very full gold.

**Nose** A hint of sherry. Nutty. Faint peat? Very appetising.

**Body** Light, smooth, silky.

**Palate** Nutty dryness and a toffeeish (but elusive, light and clean) sweetness, beautifully balanced.

**Finish** Gentle, with a clean sweetness, becoming perfumy. Lingering, very warm.

### SCORE 77

# GLEN ALBYN

**Producer** United Distillers
**Region** Highlands   **District** Speyside (Inverness)

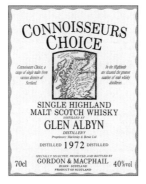

HE CITY OF INVERNESS is regarded as the capital of the Highlands. Despite a distillery being on the western edge of the region, it would perhaps qualify for the appellation nevertheless. The city did have three distilleries, all dating from the 1800s, but they were closed in the 1980s. In Brian Townsend's book, *Scotch Missed*, there is an evocative waterside photograph of Glen Albyn distillery before it was demolished to make way for a supermarket. Its whisky went for blending, and was never renowned as a single malt, but surviving stocks show it to be a pleasant drink.

**House style** Flowery, dry. Aperitif.

**GLEN ALBYN 1972, 40 vol, Connoisseurs Choice**

| |
|---|
| **Colour** Amber. |
| **Nose** Peaty, smoky, light sherry. |
| **Body** Medium, firm. |
| **Palate** Very clean and long. Initially cleanly dry, then nutty and sherryish notes emerging. |
| **Finish** Surprisingly fresh, with peaty and oaky notes. |

### SCORE 74

**Other versions of Glen Albyn**
A Master of Malt 12-year-old at 43 vol was almost white, and remarkably clean and fresh, with a touch of soapiness on the nose. SCORE 70. A Signatory 1974 at 58 vol was spirity on the nose, but perfumy and flowery in the palate. SCORE 70. A 1975 at cask strength from Oddbins was very similar in style, but perhaps a little smoother. SCORE 71.

# GLENALLACHIE

**Producer** Pernod/Campbell
**Region** Highlands **District** Speyside

GLENALLACHIE
**12** YEARS OLD
Single Highland Malt
Scotch Whisky
DISTILLED AND BOTTLED IN SCOTLAND
THE GLENALLACHIE DISTILLERY CO. LTD.
LEITH · SCOTLAND
75 cl 40% vol.

**G** LENALLACHIE IS IN THE HEART of Speyside, near Aberlour. A dam and a small waterfall soften the exterior of the functional modern distillery building. It was built in 1967 primarily to contribute malt to the Mackinlay blends, owned at that time by Scottish and Newcastle Breweries. In 1985, the distillery and 11 other Mackinlay businesses were acquired by Invergordon. The distillery was temporarily closed in the late 1980s, then acquired and reopened by Campbell Distillers at the end of the decade. Glenallachie (pronounced "Glen-alec-y") is a superb example of a subtle, complex Speyside whisky of the delicate type. It has never been well known as a single malt, and is not currently being bottled, which is a shame – it deserves a greater reputation.

**House style** Complex, subtle, delicate. Aperitif.

| GLENALLACHIE 12-year-old, 40 vol |
|---|
| An elegant and graceful pre-dinner companion. |
| **Colour** Very pale. |
| **Nose** Fragrant, lightly sweet and malty. |
| **Body** Light but firm. |
| **Palate** Beautifully clean, smooth and delicate. |
| **Finish** Starts sweet and develops towards a long perfumy finish. |

SCORE 76

# GLENBURGIE

**Producer** Allied Distillers
**Region** Highlands **District** Speyside (Findhorn)

**L**YING AT THE WATERSHED of the Findhorn between Forres and Elgin, this distillery produces distinctively herbal-tasting malts that contribute to the Ballantine blends but are hard to find as single malts. There have been official bottlings at five years old, but they are not regularly available. Independent bottlings can also be found at other ages. A distillery was founded on the site at Alves in 1829, but it subsequently fell into disuse. It was revived in 1878 and extended in 1958. At that time, two Lomond stills were added, but the whisky made in these stills has never been officially released. Independent bottlings were made under the name Glencraig and these can still be found, although stocks are finite. The Lomond stills were removed in the early 1980s.

**House style** Oily, fruity. Aperitif.

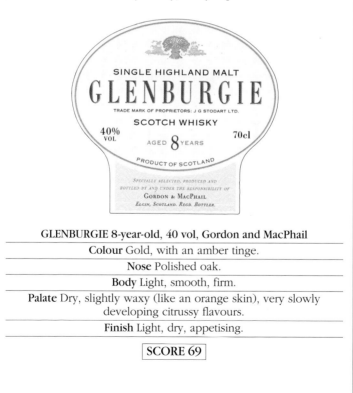

SINGLE HIGHLAND MALT

## GLENBURGIE

TRADE MARK OF PROPRIETORS: J G STODART LTD.

**SCOTCH WHISKY**

40% VOL    AGED 8 YEARS    70cl

PRODUCT OF SCOTLAND

SPECIALLY SELECTED, PRODUCED AND BOTTLED BY AND UNDER THE RESPONSIBILITY OF
GORDON & MACPHAIL
ELGIN, SCOTLAND. REGD. BOTTLER.

| GLENBURGIE 8-year-old, 40 vol, Gordon and MacPhail |
| --- |
| **Colour** Gold, with an amber tinge. |
| **Nose** Polished oak. |
| **Body** Light, smooth, firm. |
| **Palate** Dry, slightly waxy (like an orange skin), very slowly developing citrussy flavours. |
| **Finish** Light, dry, appetising. |

### SCORE 69

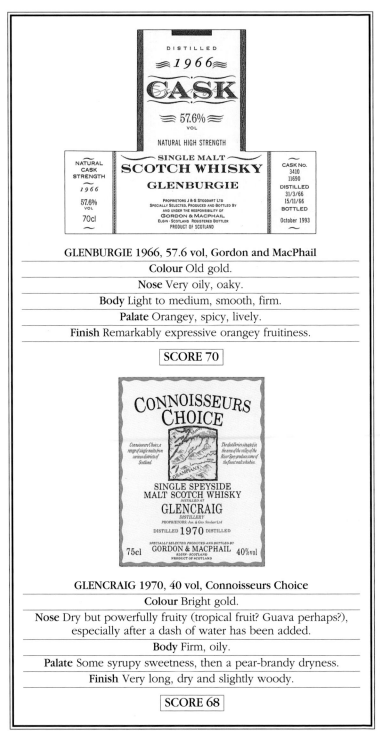

**GLENBURGIE 1966, 57.6 vol, Gordon and MacPhail**

| | |
|---|---|
| **Colour** Old gold. | |

**Colour** Old gold.

**Nose** Very oily, oaky.

**Body** Light to medium, smooth, firm.

**Palate** Orangey, spicy, lively.

**Finish** Remarkably expressive orangey fruitiness.

SCORE 70

**GLENCRAIG 1970, 40 vol, Connoisseurs Choice**

**Colour** Bright gold.

**Nose** Dry but powerfully fruity (tropical fruit? Guava perhaps?), especially after a dash of water has been added.

**Body** Firm, oily.

**Palate** Some syrupy sweetness, then a pear-brandy dryness.

**Finish** Very long, dry and slightly woody.

SCORE 68

# GLENCADAM

**Producer** Allied Distillers
**Region** Highlands **District** Eastern Highlands

**T**HIS WELL-TENDED DISTILLERY is just outside the ancient city and market town of Brechin, on the east coast. The distillery was founded in 1825 and extensively modernised in 1959. It has been associated with Ballantine's and Stewart's Cream of the Barley blends. The latter seems appropriate as Glencadam is an unusually creamy malt. It is bottled by Gordon and MacPhail. There is also a limited edition bottling from Stewart's in a crystal decanter.

**House style** Creamy. With dessert, or after dinner.

GLENCADAM 1974, 40 vol, Connoisseurs Choice

| | |
|---|---|
| **Colour** Full. | |
| **Nose** Smoky-fruity. | |
| **Body** Full, creamy. | |
| **Palate** Fresh, with some malty, buttery sweetness. | |
| **Finish** Warming. | |

SCORE 68

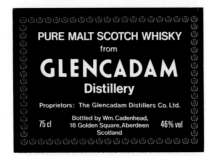

**GLENCADAM 21-year-old, 46 vol, Cadenhead**

**Colour** Full gold.

**Nose** Powerful, aromatic, smoky-fruity.

**Body** Full, drying on the tongue.

**Palate** Sweet. Strawberries and ice-cream.

**Finish** Warming, notes of bourbon.

SCORE 68

# GLEN DEVERON

**Producer** William Lawson Distillers
**Region** Highlands **District** Speyside (Deveron)

A NEOPHYTE WISHING TO LEARN the true aroma and taste of malt could do worse than work for a few evenings on a bottle of Glen Deveron. This is a clean, uncluttered, malty whisky that is very easy to drink and enjoy. It is also a single malt that is becoming more readily available as Glen Deveron 12-year-old. The Deveron is the river, valley and district on the eastern edge of Speyside. The distillery, on the banks of the river, is called Macduff and looks across the river to the town of Banff. The whisky appears under the name Macduff in some independent bottlings. The distillery was built in 1962 and is operated by William Lawson Distillers who have links through General Beverage with the international Martini and Rossi group. The malt no doubt finds it way into the William Lawson's blend.

**House style** Malty. Restorative or after dinner.

GLEN DEVERON 12-year-old, 40 vol

**Colour** Gold.

**Nose** Hints of sherry and sweet maltiness in a fresh, appetising aroma.

**Body** Light to medium, but notably smooth.

**Palate** Full, very clean, maltiness.

**Finish** Malty dryness. Quick but pleasantly warming.

SCORE 75

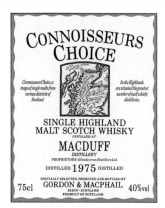

**MACDUFF 1975, 40 vol, Connoisseurs Choice**

**Colour** Amber.

**Nose** Hints of sherry (fino?).

**Body** Light to medium.

**Palate** Slightly sulphury.

**Finish** Quick.

### SCORE 70

**MACDUFF 21-year-old, 55.5 vol, James MacArthur**

**Colour** Yellowy gold.

**Nose** More sherry than colour suggests. Hint of sweet maltiness.

**Body** Light to medium, but very smooth and oily.

**Palate** Lots of flavour development. Soft and malty, moving to a sappy dryness, then a flowery sweetness.

**Finish** A little longer.

### SCORE 76

# GLENDRONACH

**Producer** Allied Distillers
**Region** Highlands **District** Speyside (Deveron)

**M**ALT LOVERS MAY STILL find on the shelf a choice between The Glendronach Original, which was matured in plain wood, and a wholly sherry-aged version, both at 12 years old. Each method of maturation is indicated on the label. It is very interesting to compare these two versions, although the latter has now been withdrawn (the company decided that its very heavy sherry character was too dominant). Both versions have now been replaced by The Glendronach Traditional, which is intended to marry the virtues of each. Some of the whisky in the bottle has been matured in plain wood and a smaller proportion in sherry casks. Plain wood means that the wood has previously been used for Scotch whisky, although it may have enjoyed an early period maturing Bourbon or sherry. In palate, the Traditional is slightly softer and sweeter than the Original, but far less dark and caramel-like than the sherry-aged version. The Glendronach distillery at Forgue, east of Huntly, is south of the River Deveron and on the very edge of Speyside. It was founded in 1826 and acquired by Teacher's in 1960. It has floor maltings and coal-fired stills.

**House style** Smooth, malty, sherryish. After dinner.

*The Glendronach distillery is set in rich Aberdeenshire farming country.*

**GLENDRONACH Traditional, 12-year-old, 40 vol**

**Colour** Bright, full amber. Very attractive.

**Nose** Sweetish sherry notes, lots of malt, some heather.

**Body** Medium to full. Very smooth, slight chewiness.

**Palate** Light but definite sherry, a touch of oak, malt, heather and faint peat.

**Finish** Longer, more spicy, drier.

SCORE 76

**GLENDRONACH Original, 12-year-old, 43 vol**

**Colour** Gold.

**Nose** Dry, with a hint of sherry and lots of maltiness.

**Body** Medium to full. Very smooth and slightly syrupy.

**Palate** Well-balanced by heathery dryness.

**Finish** Big development of flavour, with clean, fruity, perfumy notes.

SCORE 75

**GLENDRONACH Matured in sherry casks, 12-year-old, 40 vol**

**Colour** Very deep amber.

**Nose** Intense sherry (sweet oloroso?).

**Body** Very rich and luscious.

**Palate** A good balance of sherry character and maltiness. Some caramel-like sweetness, although by no means overpowering.

**Finish** Very long, with some dryness.

SCORE 77

**GLENDRONACH 18-year-old, 43 vol**
(There has also been a limited edition at 19 years old.)

**Colour** A bright, extremely deep amber.

**Nose** Plenty of sherry, but also a burnt-toffee dryness and a hint of smoke.

**Body** Smooth, slightly drying.

**Palate** Starts with burnt-toffee dryness, moves to malty sweetness, then to sherry.

**Finish** Long, smooth, warming, with some toffeeish dryness.

SCORE 79

# GLENDULLAN

**Producer** United Distillers
**Region** Highland   **District** Speyside (Dufftown)

**A**N UNDERRATED and not especially well-known malt that is worth sampling. Supplied to King Edward VII in 1902 (this fact was proclaimed for some years on its casks), Glendullan is one of several malts associated with the Old Parr blends, which originated from Macdonald Greenlees. A bottling under the Macdonald Greenlees name has a good dash of sherry. A newer bottling in the United Distillers Flora and Fauna series has more distillery character. The distillery was founded in 1897 and expanded in 1972.

**House style** Perfumy, fruity. Digestif.

**GLENDULLAN 12-year-old, 43 vol**
A big assertive after-dinner malt; or put it in a hip-flask.

| | |
|---|---|
| **Colour** Amber. | |

**Colour** Amber.

**Nose** Some sherry, malty, lightly perfumy and fruity.

**Body** Medium to full. Smooth, firm and silky.

**Palate** Powerful, dry and malty, with perfumy, fruity notes developing.

**Finish** Firm, long, warming.

SCORE 75

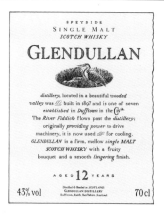

SPEYSIDE
SINGLE MALT
*SCOTCH WHISKY*

# GLENDULLAN

*distillery*, located in a beautiful *wooded
valley* was built in 1897 and is one of seven
*established* in *Dufftown* in the 19th
The *River Fiddich* flows past the *distillery*;
originally *providing power* to drive
machinery, it is now used for cooling.
*GLENDULLAN* is a firm, mellow *single MALT
SCOTCH WHISKY* with a fruity
bouquet and a smooth *lingering* finish.

AGED **12** YEARS

Distilled & Bottled in *SCOTLAND*
GLENDULLAN DISTILLERY
Dufftown, Keith, Banffshire, Scotland

43% vol                    70 cl

### GLENDULLAN 12-year-old, 43 vol, Flora and Fauna
Starts modestly, but the finish is remarkable. A malt to savour.

**Colour** Almost white, with just a tinge of gold.

**Nose** Light, dry maltiness. Hint of fruit.

**Body** Medium, firm, silky.

**Palate** Dry start, becoming malty, nutty, perfumy and lightly fruity.

**Finish** Extraordinarily perfumy and long.

### SCORE 75

PRODUCT OF SCOTLAND
**SINGLE MALT SCOTCH WHISKY**
from

# Glendullan-Glenlivet
**Distillery**

**Proprietors: Macdonald Greenlees Ltd.**

75 cl    Bottled by Wm. Cadenhead,    46% vol
18 Golden Square, Aberdeen
Scotland

### GLENDULLAN 22-year-old, 46 vol, Cadenhead

**Colour** Pale gold.

**Nose** Dry, assertive.

**Body** Medium to full, drying on the tongue.

**Palate** More sweetness and perfume. Less well-balanced.

**Finish** Perfumy, warming.

### SCORE 74

# GLEN ELGIN

**Producer** United Distillers
**Region** Highlands  **District** Speyside (Lossie)

**W**HERE THE RIVER LOSSIE approaches the malt whisky town of Elgin, there are no fewer than eight distilleries within a few miles. Glen Elgin is not the nearest to the town whose name it bears, but close enough. There are some excellent whiskies in this stretch of country, and the sweetish Glen Elgin is one of them. The distillery was founded in 1898–1900, and rebuilt and extended in 1964. The malt is an important component of the White Horse blended whisky. Glen Elgin has been available as a 12-year-old single malt in an official bottling for some years. In 1991, a new official bottling was introduced, still at 12 years old, but with no age statement on the label. The new bottling seems fractionally paler and slightly less smoky in the nose, with some dryish sherry notes.

**House style** Honey and tangerines. Restorative or after dinner.

---

**GLEN ELGIN, no age statement, 43 vol**

**Colour** Medium gold.

**Nose** Heather honey.

**Body** Light to medium.

**Palate** Dryish flowery start; becoming sweet, honeyish, clean and malty; developing a dash of tangerine-like fruitiness.

**Finish** Smooth, becoming drier again, with late notes of smoke and sherry.

---

### SCORE 76

**Other versions of Glen Elgin**

A Cadenhead 22-year-old at 50.1 vol had a greeny-gold colour, a powerful heather-honey aroma, a smooth body, a sweet, honeyish palate and a drier, fruity finish.
SCORE 76.

# GLENESK

**Producer** United Distillers
**Region** Highlands   **District** Eastern Highlands

**GLENESK**

YEARS **12** OLD
**SINGLE MALT**
HIGHLAND SCOTCH WHISKY

*Wm Sanderson ston, Ltd.*
Distillers, South Queensferry, Scotland
Bottled in Scotland
**40% vol   75 cl**

LTHOUGH IT IS BOTTLED under the distillery label, this fresh, clean, lightly malty whisky can be hard to find as a single malt. Traditionally it has been a major component of the blended whisky VAT 69, bottled in South Queensferry near Edinburgh by William Sanderson. The distillery is at the mouth of the South Esk River, at Montrose. It began its life as a flax mill and became a malt distillery in 1897. It was re-equipped to produce grain whisky around the time of the Second World War, converted back to malt in the 1960s, and extended in the 1970s. It has been temporarily closed since 1985. Despite its chequered history, it has very much the look of a traditional malt distillery. Its adjoining drum-type maltings are working.

**House style** Fresh, clean, dry. Aperitif.

---

### GLENESK 12-year-old, 40 vol

| **Colour** Gold. |
|---|

| **Nose** Dry maltiness. Aromatic. Some restrained, balancing sweetness. |
|---|

| **Body** Light to medium, soft, smooth. |
|---|

| **Palate** Soft and pleasant. Dry maltiness, with some balancing notes of restrained sweetness. |
|---|

| **Finish** An aromatic, dry maltiness throughout makes for an unusual clean and fresh malt. |
|---|

| SCORE 66 |
|---|

# GLENFARCLAS

**Producer** J. and G. Grant
**Region** Highlands   **District** Speyside

O UTSTANDING MALTS, and in an unusually wide variety of ages – experienced tasters usually place the Glenfarclas malts in the top three or four from this most distinguished district. They are at the heftier end of the Speyside line-up, although they are not the very heaviest. They are also emphatically in the well-sherried style. In both respects they are less assertive than The Macallan, with which they are often compared. Glenfarclas malts are the strong, silent type: tall, dark and handsome, notably firm-bodied, but willing to reveal a sweet side to their nature. They are excellent company at any time, and especially after dinner.

Glenfarclas means "valley of the green grass". The distillery is about a mile from the Spey, and set on a cattle farm just beyond which heather-covered hills rise towards Ben Rinnes, from where the distillery's water flows. Barley is grown in the surrounding area and the distillery grew out of the farm. The site, known simply as Glenfarclas, or Rechlerich, is not far from the village of Marypark, in the Ballindalloch area.

The distillery is large and successful, but it is not part of a group. It is the business of a wholly private, family-owned company, J. and G. Grant. They are not connected (except perhaps distantly) to any of the other whisky-making Grants, and regard theirs as the most truly independent of all Scottish

**Distillery Established 1836**

distilleries. The distillery was founded in 1836, and has been in the family since 1865. Its still-house is modern, and its stills are the biggest in Speyside. A substantial proportion of the whisky is aged in first-use sherry casks, some in re-fill sherry casks and some in plain wood.

**House style** Big, malty, oaky, sherryish. After dinner.

*The Glenfarclas distillery signs itself with a flourish, together with a reminder of its great age.*

### GLENFARCLAS, no age statement, 60 vol

Known as 105° from the old British proof system. This is the strongest single malt offered by any distillery in an official bottling. Although it no longer carries an age statement, it is 8 to 10 years old. A very youthful version for such a big malt, but with all the muscle of the high proof, which is virtually cask strength.

**Colour** Bronze.

**Nose** Big and uncomplicated; raisins, butterscotch and toffee.

**Body** Full, heavy.

**Palate** Very sweet, rich nectar.

**Finish** Long, and warmed by that high proof. This is one to accompany a slice of rich fruit cake. Extra points for cheeky, youthful individuality.

### SCORE 88

### GLENFARCLAS 10-year-old, 40 vol

Elegant and quite dry for a Glenfarclas.

**Colour** Bronze.

**Nose** Big, with some sherry sweetness, but also smokiness at the back of the nose.

**Body** Characteristically firm.

**Palate** Crisp and dry at first, with the flavour filling out as it develops.

**Finish** Sweet and long.

### SCORE 86

### GLENFARCLAS 12-year-old, 43 vol
For many devotees, the most familiar face of Glenfarclas.

**Colour** Bronze.

**Nose** Drier, with a quick, big attack.

**Body** Firm, slightly oily.

**Palate** Plenty of flavour, with notes of peat-smoke.

**Finish** Long, with oaky notes, even at this relatively young age.

### SCORE 87

### GLENFARCLAS 15-year-old, 46 vol
Many enthusiasts feel that the 15-year-old most deftly demonstrates the complexity of this malt. Certainly the best-balanced Glenfarclas.

**Colour** Amber.

**Nose** Plenty of sherry, oak, maltiness, and a hint of smokiness – all the elements of a lovely, mixed bouquet.

**Body** Firm, rounded.

**Palate** Assertive, again with all the elements beautifully melded.

**Finish** Long and smooth.

### SCORE 88

### GLENFARCLAS 17-year-old, 43 vol
Mainly available in the Far East.

**Colour** Full amber

**Nose** Fuller sherry. Light, fragrant smokiness. Clean oak.

**Body** Firm, rounded.

**Palate** Firm at first, then a surge of buttery notes in the middle, moving to fruity dryness.

**Finish** Touch of bitter chocolate.

### SCORE 88

### GLENFARCLAS 21-year-old, 43 vol

**Colour** Amber.

**Nose** More sherry, greater smokiness, as well as a dash of oak. All slowly emerging as distinct notes.

**Body** Big, firm.

**Palate** Immense flavour development, with many more notes.

**Finish** Remarkably long, with lots of sherry, becoming sweetish and perfumy.

### SCORE 89

### GLENFARCLAS 25-year-old, 43 vol

More of everything. Perhaps a touch woody for purists, but a remorselessly serious after-dinner malt for others.

**Colour** Dark amber.

**Nose** Pungent, sappy.

**Body** Big, with some dryness of texture.

**Palate** The flavours are so tightly interlocked at first that the whisky appears reluctant to give up its secrets. Very slow, insistent flavour development. All the components gradually emerge, but in a drier mood.

**Finish** Long, oaky, sappy. Extra points out of respect for idiosyncratic age.

### SCORE 88

### GLENFARCLAS 30-year-old (1961), 43 vol

**Colour** Profound, refractive, amber.

**Nose** Oaky, slightly woody.

**Body** Very firm.

**Palate** Nutty and oaky.

**Finish** Oaky, sappy, peaty.

### SCORE 88

# GLENFIDDICH

**Producer** William Grant and Sons
**Region** Highlands    **District** Speyside (Dufftown)

T HE GLEN OF THE RIVER FIDDICH gives its name to the biggest-selling single malt whisky in the world. The Glenfiddich distillery lies on the small river whose name it bears, in Dufftown. The name Fiddich indicates that the river runs through the valley of the deer – hence the company's emblem: a stag.

Glenfiddich spent some time waiting to be discovered. The distillery was founded in 1886–87, and is still owned by the original family as a limited company. Nonetheless, it made an early start in the business of bottling single malts.

As a small family company, it faced intense competition from bigger names during the economic boom after the Second World War. In 1963, it decided to market its whisky as a single malt outside Scotland. For many years, companies in the industry regarded this as foolishness. The received wisdom of the whisky business was that single malts were too intense in palate for the English and other foreigners.

The vision and persistence of the company was in more than one sense single-minded. It was an example and precedent, without which few of its rivals would have been emboldened to offer themselves as bottled single malts. Devotees of the genre owe a debt of gratitude to Glenfiddich.

The early start laid the foundations for the success of Glenfiddich. The fact that it is, among malts, one of the less challenging to the palate undoubtedly helped a great deal. Glenfiddich in its usual form (no age statement, but said to be eight years old) is very easily drinkable: a light, smooth malt with a hint of fruitiness. It is labelled "Special Old Reserve". Devotees of malts who are ready for a greater challenge will find more complexity, at a price, in the elaborately packaged 18-, 21- and 30-year-old versions that are now available. In 1991, nine casks of a 50-year-old were bottled. These were sold in London at around US $5,000 each, but one fetched US $70,000 in an auction in Milan. For its age, the whisky was surprisingly rounded and chocolatey, without excessive oakiness. The company also owns the long-established Balvenie and new Kininvie malt distilleries. The principal malt may be close to the mainstream, but the distillery is full of character. Much of the original structure, in honey-and-grey stone, remains beautifully maintained, and the style has been followed in considerable new construction.

A truly traditional element is the use of coal-fired stills. The stills are small, and the whisky is principally aged in plain oak, although about ten per cent goes into sherry casks. Whisky aged in different woods is married in plain oak. Glenfiddich likes jokingly to describe its malt as "Château-bottled". The distillery is unusual in that it has its own bottling line on the premises. The only other malt distillery with bottling facilities is Springbank, where a very small line is also used for the Cadenhead range.

William Grant no longer sells whisky for blending under the Glenfiddich name, the intention being to ensure that the company can guarantee the origin of any whisky bearing this name. Like several other distillers, it feels that its label should be used only on whisky aged according to its own practices. Cadenhead, however, has marketed some older ages of single malt whisky under the name Glenfiddich-Glenlivet.

**House style** When young, a dry, fruity aperitif; when more mature, a raisiny, chocolatey after-dinner malt.

*The handsome steeply pitched roofs and traditional pagoda shape of distillery maltings at the Glenfiddich distillery.*

## GLENFIDDICH Special Old Reserve, no age statement, 40 vol

**Colour** Very pale, white wine.

**Nose** Light, fresh but sweet, appetising, fruity, pear-like.

**Body** Light, lean, firm, smooth.

**Palate** Dryish, pear-like, more fruitiness as flavour develops. A dash of water releases a hint of smokiness and some sweet, malty notes.

**Finish** Restrained, aromatic.

### SCORE 75

## GLENFIDDICH Classic, no age statement, 43 vol

**Colour** Pale gold.

**Nose** Softer. Dry maltiness, pear-skins, slight sherry and faint smokiness.

**Body** Firm, smooth.

**Palate** Smooth. Dry maltiness balanced by restrained sweetness, with slight smokiness. Flavours tightly combined.

**Finish** Smooth, dry.

### SCORE 76

*Spode presentation decanter with hand-stamped seal.*

## GLENFIDDICH 18-year-old, 43 vol

**Colour** Full gold.

**Nose** Softer, richer.

**Body** Much softer.

**Palate** Much more mellow and rounded, soft and restrained.

**Finish** Dryish. A hint of peat?

### SCORE 78

### GLENFIDDICH Excellence 18-year-old, 43 vol

This bottling seems slightly paler in colour and lighter on the nose than the 18-year-old version in the Spode decanter.

**Colour** Gold.

**Nose** Softer, more flowery.

**Body** Very smooth and well-rounded.

**Palate** Mellow, developing sweeter notes.

**Finish** Dryish, lengthening.

## SCORE 77

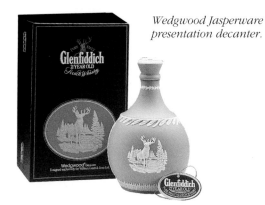

*Wedgwood Jasperware presentation decanter.*

### GLENFIDDICH 21-year-old, 43 vol

**Colour** Full gold, fractionally darker.

**Nose** Hint of sherry?

**Body** Surprisingly full.

**Palate** Complex, with both sweetness and dryness. Eventually the dry notes are more assertive, with a hint of peat.

**Finish** Still gentle, but longer.

## SCORE 81

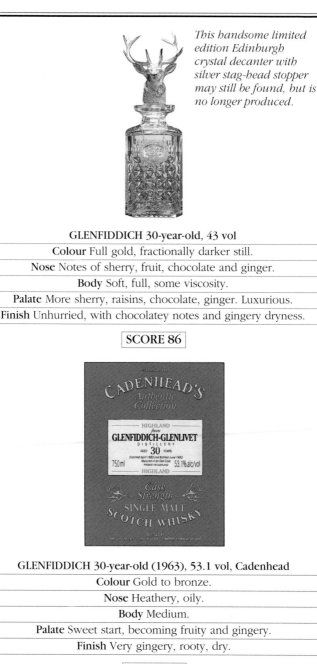

*This handsome limited edition Edinburgh crystal decanter with silver stag-head stopper may still be found, but is no longer produced.*

### GLENFIDDICH 30-year-old, 43 vol

**Colour** Full gold, fractionally darker still.

**Nose** Notes of sherry, fruit, chocolate and ginger.

**Body** Soft, full, some viscosity.

**Palate** More sherry, raisins, chocolate, ginger. Luxurious.

**Finish** Unhurried, with chocolatey notes and gingery dryness.

## SCORE 86

### GLENFIDDICH 30-year-old (1963), 53.1 vol, Cadenhead

**Colour** Gold to bronze.

**Nose** Heathery, oily.

**Body** Medium.

**Palate** Sweet start, becoming fruity and gingery.

**Finish** Very gingery, rooty, dry.

## SCORE 77

# GLEN GARIOCH

**Producer** Morrison Bowmore
**Region** Highlands **District** Eastern Highlands

**B**ETWEEN SPEYSIDE and the east coast, Glen Garioch (pronounced "Geery") is the Highland partner of the Lowland malt Auchentoshan and the island malt Bowmore. These three distilleries share an owner, and each produces excellent malts. The Glen Garioch distillery is on the road from Banff to Aberdeen, at the quaintly named town of Old Meldrum, in the sheltered Garioch valley – traditionally a grain-growing district. The distillery, founded in 1798, is a chunky, stone building that looks in parts like a village school. It is very traditional in that it has floor maltings, but innovative in the manner in which it has sought to re-use the heat generated in the distilling process. In the oldest ages of Glen Garioch is the peaty style of malt, although this character is less evident in the younger versions.

**House style** Heathery, with some peat. Aperitif, or even as an accompaniment to Scottish dishes.

### GLEN GARIOCH 1984, 40 vol

**Colour** Full gold.

**Nose** Perfumy, sweetish, heathery, very faint peat.

**Body** Medium, smooth.

**Palate** Malty, syrupy, raisiny, developing towards dryish, heathery, faintly peaty notes.

**Finish** A late surge of sweetness and heathery spiciness (some tasters have found violets).

SCORE 76

### GLEN GARIOCH 12-year-old, 40 vol

**Colour** Bronze.

**Nose** Fragrant, leafy peatiness. Touch of dry oloroso?

**Body** Medium, firm.

**Palate** Beautifully interlocked heather-honey sweetness and peat-smoky dryness.

**Finish** Echoes of both elements. Quick and warming.

SCORE 77

### GLEN GARIOCH 15-year-old, 43 vol

**Colour** Full gold.

**Nose** Good whiff of peat smoke. Very aromatic.

**Body** Medium, rich.

**Palate** Very gradual development from malty, syrupy notes through heather and perfumy smokiness.

**Finish** Very long, spicy, warming.

SCORE 79

**GLEN GARIOCH 21-year-old, 43 vol**
A robust malt that deserves to be better known.

**Colour** Pale gold.

**Nose** Definitely smoky.

**Body** Medium to full.

**Palate** Much more intense, very sweet in the middle,
and well-rounded.

**Finish** Big and very smoky, but smooth. Lots of lingering fragrance.

### SCORE 80

**Other versions of Glen Garioch**
A 17-year-old at 54.2 vol under the Caskieben label was sweet and
leafy, with some vanilla, but lacked peat. SCORE 75.
Cask-strength, sherry-aged versions sampled at the Scotch Malt
Whisky Society have been rated as majestic by tasters there.

# GLENGLASSAUGH

**Producer** Highland Distilleries
**Region** Highlands **District** Speyside (Deveron)

"**S**ACKCLOTH ... HESSIAN" proclaimed one taster, admiring the distinctive aroma of this malt. Flax, perhaps? Fresh linen? Newly-made beds? "Gorse ... broom" says another admirer. It is certainly an individualistic whisky and inspires flights of fancy – maybe it is the aroma of seaside sand dunes covered with rough grass and gorse. This is a seaside malt, produced near Portsoy, on the coast of Speyside. The distillery is between the Spey and the River Deveron. It was founded in 1875, bought by Highland Distilleries in the 1890s, and completely rebuilt in 1960. It has been temporarily mothballed since the mid-1980s. The single malt is not widely available. In some countries it carries a 12-year age statement. The whisky has also contributed to blends like The Famous Grouse, Cutty Sark and Laing's.

**House style** Grassy maltiness. Restorative or refresher.

| GLENGLASSAUGH, no age statement, 40 vol |
|---|
| **Colour** Gold. |
| **Nose** Fresh linen. |
| **Body** Light, but firm and smooth. |
| **Palate** Grassy, sweetish. |
| **Finish** Gentle, drying slightly. |

SCORE 76

## GLENGLASSAUGH 1983, 40 vol, Connoisseurs Choice

**Colour** Full gold to bronze.

**Nose** Grassy, dry, some sherry.

**Body** Light, firm, slight syrupiness.

**Palate** Drier. Flavours tightly combined, with notes of grass and peaches.

**Finish** Peach skins, grass, sea-salt.

**SCORE 76**

## GLENGLASSAUGH 15-year-old, 59 vol, Cadenhead

**Colour** Fino sherry, perhaps even paler.

**Nose** Salt, grass, pepper.

**Body** Light to medium. Firm.

**Palate** Grassy, oily, peppery, complex.

**Finish** Extraordinarily peppery, assertive, appetising.

**SCORE 76**

# GLENGOYNE

**Producer** Lang Brothers
**Region** Highlands **District** Western Highlands

 N EMINENTLY VISITABLE DISTILLERY, just over a dozen miles from the centre of Glasgow, and six or seven from Loch Lomond. Glengoyne lies in the valley of a small river that eventually flows into the loch. Sheep graze on the hills behind, and burns flow into a well-tended glen, forming a waterfall. It is said to have been established in 1833, and was earlier known as "Burn Foot" or "Glen Guin". It has been owned by Lang's since the 1870s. Since the mid-1960s, Lang's has been a subsidiary of Robertson and Baxter. That company in turn have links with Highland Distillers, whose subsidiary, Matthew Gloag, produces The Famous Grouse. Glengoyne is the only distillery to emphasise the use of unpeated malt. Its vintage editions are a particular pleasure.

**House style** Easily drinkable, but full of flavour. Restorative or after dinner.

**GLENGOYNE 10-year-old, 40 vol**

| | |
|---|---|
| **Colour** Full gold. | |
| **Nose** A fresh but very soft, warm fruitiness, with hints of malty dryness and sherry. | |
| **Body** Light to medium, smooth, rounded. | |
| **Palate** Clean, sweetish, tasty, very pleasant. | |
| **Finish** Still sweet, but drying slightly. Clean, appetising. | |

SCORE 74

**GLENGOYNE 12-year-old, 43 vol**
Very similar to the 10-year-old. A dash more of everything.

SCORE 75

## GLENGOYNE 17-year-old, 43 vol

**Colour** Full gold, with a touch of amber.

**Nose** Warm, dry. Maltiness and fruitiness. Palo cortado sherry. Cedar and oak.

**Body** Medium, very firm and smooth.

**Palate** Deep flavours. Malt, clean fruitiness, nuttiness, cedar, oak.

**Finish** Long and sherryish.

SCORE 77

## GLENGOYNE 1968, 50.3 vol

**Colour** Full gold to amber

**Nose** Beautifully balanced fragrances. Malty dryness, sherry character and juicy oak.

**Body** Medium to full. Exceptionally smooth.

**Palate** Clean, soft, rich maltiness, becoming slightly chewy as it blends into sherry.

**Finish** Long, sherryish, touches of ginger and juicy oak.

SCORE 79

# GLEN GRANT

**Producer** Seagram/Chivas
**Region** Highlands  **District** Speyside (Rothes)

**O**NE OF THE GREAT MALTS, by common consent. Glen Grant has been sold as a bottled single malt since the first decade of this century. It was well known in Scotland long before pioneers like Glenfiddich began to open up the English and international markets. Glen Grant is among the world's biggest-selling single malts, but much of its sales are in the younger ages, especially in the important Italian market. Glen Grant combines easy drinkability with a dash of distinction. This is especially true of the 10-year-old version. The version with no age statement, which is the principal Glen Grant in Britain, generally contains malt of not less than eight or nine years old. These two, and the 15-year-old, have undoubtedly introduced many instant converts to the pursuit of single malts. There are older versions from independent bottlers, including sherryish vintages under the Prime Malt label in America. Glen Grant was founded in 1840, and some of the original buildings remain. The distillery is set around a small courtyard, with turreted and gabled offices in the "Scottish baronial" style, probably dating from the 1880s. Some of the stills are coal-fired.

**House style** Herbal, with notes of hazelnut. In younger ages, an aperitif; with sherry age, after dinner.

*The Glen Grant distillery is tucked away at the end of the main street of Rothes, one of the whisky towns of the Spey Valley.*

### GLEN GRANT 5-year-old, 40 vol

**Colour** Very pale, white wine.

**Nose** Light, dry fruitiness, spirity.

**Body** Light, slightly sticky, almost resiny.

**Palate** Spirity. Pear-brandy.

**Finish** Fruity, quick.

### GLEN GRANT, no age statement, 40 vol

**Colour** Gold.

**Nose** Fruity, flowery, nutty, faintly spirity.

**Body** Light but firm.

**Palate** Dry, slightly astringent at first, becoming soft and nutty.

**Finish** Herbal.

SCORE 74

**GLEN GRANT 10-year-old, 43 vol**
Glen Grant character without an obvious intervention of sherry.

**Colour** Full gold.

**Nose** Still dry, but much softer, with some sweetness.

**Body** Light to medium.

**Palate** Lightly sweet start, quickly becoming nutty and very dry.

**Finish** Very dry, with herbal notes.

SCORE 76

GLEN GRANT 15-year-old, 40 vol, Gordon and MacPhail

**Colour** Medium amber.

**Nose** Some sherry.

**Body** Light to medium.

**Palate** Sherryish, soft and nutty, dry.

**Finish** Mellow, warming.

SCORE 80

### GLEN GRANT 13-year-old, 55.1 vol, Cadenhead

**Colour** Greeny-gold.

**Nose** Dry, flowery.

**Body** Light but firm, with some viscosity.

**Palate** Sweet, nutty.

**Finish** Dry, touches of vanilla, lingering herbal notes, with appetising bitterness.

SCORE 76

### GLEN GRANT 16-year-old, 46 vol, Cadenhead

**Colour** Fino sherry.

**Nose** Appetisingly fruity. Dessert apples? Hazelnut?

**Body** Light to medium, soft.

**Palate** Hazelnuts. Grassy. Bamboo shoots?

**Finish** Grassy, flowery.

SCORE 77

**GLEN GRANT 21-year-old, 40 vol, Gordon and MacPhail**
Take it slowly, and appreciate the subtlety and development.

**Colour** Full amber-red.

**Nose** Lots of sherry.

**Body** Medium, soft.

**Palate** Sherryish sweetness at first, then malt and grassy-peaty notes, finally the nutty Glen Grant dryness.

**Finish** Lingering, flowery.

SCORE 81

**GLEN GRANT 23-year-old, 46 vol, Cadenhead**

**Colour** As red as a ripe apple.

**Nose** Powerful sherry. Appetising.

**Body** Medium, soft.

**Palate** Lots of sherry, but the nutty dryness of the whisky still fights through.

**Finish** Overwhelmingly dry. Woody. Astringent.

SCORE 69

**GLEN GRANT 25-year-old, 40 vol, Gordon and MacPhail**
Not so much chess as wrist-wrestling, with the sherry coming out on top. A robust version.

**Colour** Dark.

**Nose** Lots of sherry.

**Body** Medium, firm.

**Palate** Dry oloroso character at first, then nutty dryness. A lot of depth.

**Finish** Deep, flowery, peaty.

SCORE 81

**GLEN GRANT 26-year-old, 46 vol, Cadenhead**

**Colour** Ripe plum? Almost opaque.

**Nose** Powerful sherry.

**Body** Medium, soft.

**Palate** Overwhelmed by the sherry.

**Finish** Astringent.

SCORE 66

**GLEN GRANT 1965, 40 vol, Gordon and MacPhail**

**Colour** Very deep gold.

**Nose** Sherryish nuttiness, herbal notes.

**Body** Medium, smooth.

**Palate** Sherryish, lightly creamy, remarkable hazelnut character.

**Finish** Soothing, creamy, savoury.

SCORE 82

**GLEN GRANT 1964, 46 vol, Signatory**

**Colour** Amber-red.

**Nose** Sherry, nutty dryness.

**Body** Medium, smooth.

**Palate** Sherryish, nutty, with some sappy woodiness.

**Finish** Gently dry, with some sherryish, woody notes.

**SCORE 79**

**GLEN GRANT 1960, 40 vol, Gordon and MacPhail**
Less sherry, but a beautifully mellow, mature malt.

**Colour** Medium amber.

**Nose** Some sherry.

**Body** Medium.

**Palate** Sherryish and sweet, with mellow nuttiness.

**Finish** Very long and sweet, with gradual development of gentle dryness.

**SCORE 81**

# GLEN KEITH

**Producer** Seagram/Chivas
**Region** Highlands   **District** Speyside (Strathisla)

EAGRAM OWNS TWO DISTILLERIES next door to one
another in the town of Keith, on the River Isla. One
simply takes the name of the district, Strathisla, the
other is Glen Keith, which was established on the site of a
corn mill in 1957. It was the first new malt distillery to have
been founded in Scotland since a previous boom in late
Victorian times. Glen Keith had the first gas-fired still in
Scotland and pioneered the use of computers in the industry.
Its malt had its first official bottling in 1994. Like several malts
from this district, it has a dry suggestion of fresh wood.

**House style** Gingery, rooty, tart. Before dinner.

| GLEN KEITH 10-year-old, 43 vol |
|---|
| **Colour** Solid gold. |
| **Nose** Ginger cake, cedar, oak. |
| **Body** Medium. |
| **Palate** Sweet, chewy, gingery. Not complex, but very approachable and pleasantly drinkable. |
| **Finish** Gingery, fruity, with very late tartness. |

### SCORE 73

# GLENKINCHIE

**Producer** United Distillers
**Region** Lowlands **District** Eastern Lowlands

**G**LENKINCHIE IS NEAR the village of Pencaitland, about 15 miles from Edinburgh, between the soft, green Lammermuir Hills and the small coastal resorts where the Firth of Forth meets the sea. It is in the glen of the Kinchie, a tributary of the Scottish River Tyne (not to be confused with the English one of the same name). The distillery, which has its own bowling green, is set in farmland. In the 1940s and 1950s, the distillery manager bred prize-winning cattle, feeding them on the spent grain. In 1968, the former floor maltings were turned into a museum of malt whisky. Among the exhibits is a beautifully crafted model of the distillery which was built in 1924 by the firm of Basset-Lowke, better known for their model steam engines. It was constructed for the 1924 Empire Exhibition at Wembley, London. The distillery was founded in the 1830s and largely rebuilt between the two World Wars. Its whisky was launched as a bottled single in the "Classic Malts" range in 1988–89.

**House style** Flowery start, complex flavours and a dry finish. A restorative, especially after a walk in the hills.

| GLENKINCHIE 10-year-old, 43 vol |
| --- |
| **Colour** Gold. |
| **Nose** Soft, very sweetly aromatic, grassy sweetness. |
| **Body** Light to medium, some viscosity. |
| **Palate** A very clean, grassy sweetness. Smooth, well-defined, with lots of flavour development. |
| **Finish** Becoming spicy: cinnamon, ginger? Gentle, warming, dryish. |

**SCORE 76**

**GLENKINCHIE 21-year-old, 46 vol, Cadenhead**

**Colour** Gold.

**Nose** Aromatic.

**Body** Light to medium, soft.

**Palate** Sweet, grassy.

**Finish** Grassy, aromatic.

SCORE 76

**GLENKINCHIE 1974, 40 vol, Connoisseurs Choice**
Probably bottled at more than 10 years old, but the extra age does
not seem to have made a lot of difference.

**Colour** Full gold.

**Nose** Suggestion of hickory smoke.

**Body** Light to medium, firm.

**Palate** Sweet, grassy, faintly smoky.

**Finish** Longer.

SCORE 76

# THE GLENLIVET

**Producer** Seagram/Chivas
**Region** Highlands   **District** Speyside (Livet)

W HAT GRANDE CHAMPAGNE is to Cognac, the glen of the River Livet is to Speyside. The only whisky allowed to call itself "The Glenlivet" is historically the most famous Speyside malt. The definite article is restricted even further in that it appears on only the official bottlings from the owning company of The Glenlivet distillery, Seagram. These are branded as The Glenlivet, with the legend "Distilled by George & J. G. Smith" in small type at the bottom of the label, referring to the company that was set up by the father and son who originally founded the distillery.

The independent bottlers Gordon and MacPhail have made something of a speciality of older and vintage-dated examples of The Glenlivet, in a variety of alcoholic strengths; these are identified as George & J. G. Smith's Glenlivet Whisky. This range changes according to availability.

The glen of the Livet is also the home of two other malt distilleries: the unconnected Tamnavulin, and Braes of Glenlivet, which is also owned by Seagram. In the adjoining Avon valley, the Tomintoul distillery is also generally regarded as belonging to the Livet district. It is, indeed, in the parish of Glenlivet. All of these distilleries use the subtitle "Glenlivet" on their labels as an appellation of district. So, stretching a point, do about a dozen from other parts of Speyside. This practice, which has declined somewhat, dates from the glen's pioneering position in commercial whisky production. Merchants in the cities wanted whisky "from Glenlivet" because that was the first specific district of production that they knew by name.

The malts that are produced in and immediately around the glen are all delicate and elegant. These characteristics are sometimes regarded as being the "glen" style. The malt from Braes of Glenlivet is light, honeyish and flowery. Of its neighbours, Tamnavulin is lightest in body, and Tomintoul in palate. Within this style of delicate, elegant malts, The Glenlivet has the most body and definition.

Opinion is divided as to how much its renown derives from history and how much from its character, but the latter should not be underrated. In blindfold tastings, it shows itself to be a complex malt. It is distilled from water with a dash of hardness, and a mix of lightly and well-peated malts. About a third of the whisky is said to be matured in sherry wood.

Just as Grande Champagne rests on soil that grows the grapes best suited to Cognac, so the glen of the Livet has clean spring water that makes especially delicate whiskies. Among the distilling districts, it is the one most deeply set into the mountains. Its water rises from granite, and frequently flows underground for many miles. The mountain setting also provides for the weather that whisky-makers like. When distilling is in progress, the condensers work most effectively if cooled by very cold water, and in a climate to match.

The location also favoured illicit production in the days when commercial distilling was banned, and is a significant reason for the renown of the glen. There are said to have been a couple of hundred illicit stills in the wild mountain country around the Livet in the late 1700s and early 1800s. The district was also a haven for whisky-smugglers on their way over the mountains to the bigger cities and ports in the Midlands and south of Scotland.

At that time, partly because of grain shortages but also for reasons of political vindictiveness, the Highlanders were permitted to distill only on a domestic scale. The modern distilling industry began after the Duke of Gordon proposed more accommodating legislation. One of his tenants, already working outside the law, was the first to apply for a new licence in 1824. This enterprising character was from a family variously known by the Scottish name "Gow" and the

*These pictures, which date from the mid-1920s, show the fermenting vessels, above, the stills, top right, and filling of barrels, right, at Glenlivet. Much of the equipment remains the same today.*

English-sounding "Smith". It has over the years been thought that the family had supported Bonnie Prince Charlie, but recent research suggests that this was not the case. George Smith founded the distillery that became The Glenlivet. His son, John Gordon Smith, assisted and succeeded him.

After distilling on two other sites nearby, the Smiths moved in 1858 to the present location. In 1880, the exclusive designation "The Glenlivet" was granted in a test case. The company remained independent until 1935 and was acquired by Seagram in 1977.

Not far from the hamlet of Glenlivet, the distillery stands at a point where the grassy valley is already beginning to steepen towards the mountains. Some original buildings remain, and the offices occupy a handsome 1920s house. Far from its mountain home, and helped by the marketing power of Seagram, The Glenlivet has become the biggest-selling single malt in the large American market.

**House style** Flowery, fruity, peachy. Aperitif.

### THE GLENLIVET 12-year-old, 40 vol

**Colour** Pale gold.

**Nose** Remarkably flowery, clean and soft.

**Body** Light to medium, firm, smooth.

**Palate** Flowery, peachy, notes of vanilla, delicate balance between sweetness and malty dryness.

**Finish** Restrained, long, gently warming.

SCORE 85

## THE GLENLIVET 18-year-old, 43 vol

**Colour** Deep gold.

**Nose** Depth of flowery aromas, some sweetness and a hint of sherry.

**Body** Firm, smooth.

**Palate** Flowery and sweet at first, then developing peach-stone nuttiness.

**Finish** Dry, appetising. Very long, with interplay of sweet and bitter flavours.

### SCORE 87

## THE GLENLIVET 21-year-old, 43 vol

**Colour** Full amber.

**Nose** Emphatic sherry character.

**Body** Soft, medium.

**Palate** At first, very sherryish indeed, with an oloroso character. As the palate develops, that flowery-spicy note becomes strongly evident.

**Finish** Again, lots of sherry.

### SCORE 88

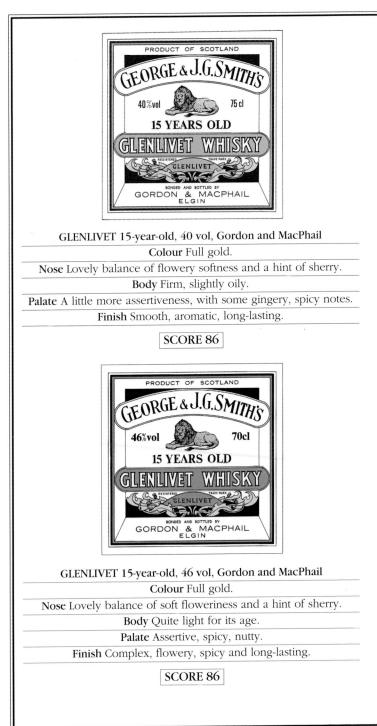

**GLENLIVET 15-year-old, 40 vol, Gordon and MacPhail**

**Colour** Full gold.

**Nose** Lovely balance of flowery softness and a hint of sherry.

**Body** Firm, slightly oily.

**Palate** A little more assertiveness, with some gingery, spicy notes.

**Finish** Smooth, aromatic, long-lasting.

SCORE 86

**GLENLIVET 15-year-old, 46 vol, Gordon and MacPhail**

**Colour** Full gold.

**Nose** Lovely balance of soft floweriness and a hint of sherry.

**Body** Quite light for its age.

**Palate** Assertive, spicy, nutty.

**Finish** Complex, flowery, spicy and long-lasting.

SCORE 86

### GLENLIVET 21-year-old, 40 vol, Gordon and MacPhail

**Colour** Full gold.

**Nose** Earthy, sherryish (fino or amontillado?)

**Body** Soft.

**Palate** Sherryish, with a flowery-spicy balance eventually emerging. A dash of herbal, leafy, peaty smokiness.

**Finish** Smooth, long-lasting.

**SCORE 87**

### GLENLIVET 1961, 40 vol, Gordon and MacPhail

**Colour** Very full gold.

**Nose** Well-balanced, fragrant, complex, with some smokiness.

**Body** Soft.

**Palate** Sherryish, with long flavour development and some smokiness.

**Finish** Big, long, warming.

**SCORE 88**

### GLENLIVET 29-year-old (1963), 52.2 vol, Signatory

**Colour** Full gold.

**Nose** Very flowery, hints of peat and smoke.

**Body** Firm.

**Palate** Flowery, nutty, some bitterness.

**Finish** Very flowery, aromatic and long.

**SCORE 87**

# GLENLOCHY

**Producer** United Distillers
**Region** Highlands **District** Western Highlands

T HE LOCHY IS A RIVER that flows through the town of Fort William, at the foot of Ben Nevis. Fort William has two distilleries: one, Ben Nevis, is in operation; the other, Glenlochy, is not. Glenlochy was built in the 1890s and has changed little over the decades. It passed to the Distillers Company Limited in 1953, lost its railway spur in the 1970s, and was closed in 1983. It has been partly dismantled and seems unlikely to reopen. Its whisky can still be found in independent bottlings, and sometimes from the Scotch Malt Whisky Society. One sophisticated and geographically precise taster found that it reminded him of Lebanese hashish.

**House style** Peaty, firm-bodied. Book-at-bedtime.

**GLENLOCHY 1974, 40 vol, Connoisseurs Choice**

| **Colour** Full gold. |
|---|
| **Nose** Light, dry, smoky, peaty. |
| **Body** Light to medium, firm, oily. |
| **Palate** Light at first, dry, becoming oily, developing towards peaty notes. |
| **Finish** Peaty, powerful, but over quite quickly. |

**SCORE 70**

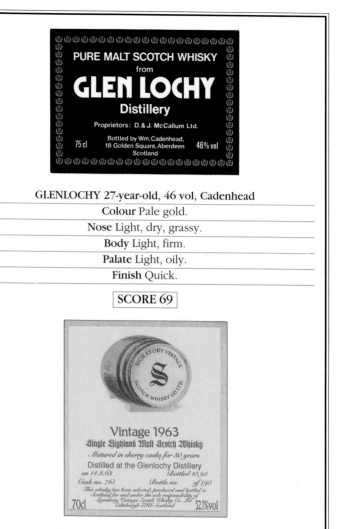

**GLENLOCHY 27-year-old, 46 vol, Cadenhead**

**Colour** Pale gold.

**Nose** Light, dry, grassy.

**Body** Light, firm.

**Palate** Light, oily.

**Finish** Quick.

SCORE 69

**GLENLOCHY 1963, 52.1 vol, Signatory**

**Colour** Pale amber.

**Nose** Peaty, oaky.

**Body** Peaty, oaky, sappy, some sherry.

**Palate** Peaty, oaky, some sherryish sweetness.

**Finish** Robust, but with some length.

SCORE 69

# GLENLOSSIE

**Producer** United Distillers
**Region** Highlands   **District** Speyside (Lossie)

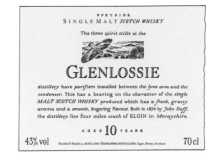

**S**PEYSIDE
SINGLE MALT *SCOTCH WHISKY*

The three *spirit stills* at the

## GLENLOSSIE

*distillery* have *purifiers* installed between the *lyne arm* and the *condenser*. This has a bearing on the *character* of the *single MALT SCOTCH WHISKY* produced which has a *fresh, grassy* aroma and a *smooth,* lingering flavour. Built in 1876 by *John Duff,* the *distillery* lies four miles *south* of ELGIN in *Morayshire.*

AGED **10** YEARS

43% vol          Distilled & Bottled in SCOTLAND. GLENLOSSIE DISTILLERY, Elgin, Moray, Scotland          70cl

**S**ANDALWOOD, PRIVET? Both have been nosed in this aromatic malt, now available as a single. The distillery, in the valley of the Lossie, south of Elgin, was built in 1876, reconstructed 20 years later, and extended in 1962. Its memorabilia include a horse-drawn fire-engine. Next door is the Mannochmore distillery, built in 1971, closed briefly in the 1980s, but now producing again.

**House style** Flowery, dry, grassy. Aperitif.

**GLENLOSSIE 10-year-old, 43 vol, Flora and Fauna**

| |
|---|
| **Colour** Fino sherry. |
| **Nose** Fresh. Grass, heather, sandalwood. |
| **Body** Light to medium. Soft, smooth. |
| **Palate** Malty, dryish at first, developing a range of sweeter, perfumy, spicy notes. |
| **Finish** Spicy. |

**SCORE 76**

**Other versions of Glenlossie**
A Gordon and MacPhail 1971 at 40 vol was sherryish, but still with plenty of distillery character. SCORE 76. A Scotch Malt Whisky Society 1981 at 55.3 vol was somewhere between the two. SCORE 76.

# GLEN MHOR

**Producer** United Distillers
**Region** Highlands   **District** Speyside (Inverness)

**P**URISTS PRONOUNCE IT the Gaelic way, "Glen Vawr". The distillery, built in 1892 in Inverness and demolished in 1986, was one of several at which the poet, novelist and pioneering whisky-writer Neil Gunn worked as an exciseman. In *Scotch Missed,* Brian Townsend writes that Gunn was inspired by Glen Mhor to let slip his observation that "until a man has had the luck to chance upon a perfectly matured malt, he does not really know what whisky is". Even in Gunn's day, Glen Mhor could be found as a single malt, and casks still find their way into independent bottlings.

**House style** Aromatic, treacly. At older ages, voluptuous.
After dinner.

GLEN MHOR 8-year-old, 40 vol, Gordon and MacPhail

| | |
|---|---|
| **Colour** Gold. | |

**Colour** Gold.

**Nose** "Sweet shop" aroma; treacle toffee?

**Body** Light, soft.

**Palate** Sweetly nutty, with some burnt caramel, dryness.

**Finish** Light, aromatic, surprisingly refreshing.

**SCORE 64**

**GLEN MHOR 15-year-old, 40 vol, Gordon and MacPhail**

**Colour** Amber.

**Nose** Sweet, oloroso sherry.

**Body** Light, soft, smooth.

**Palate** Enjoyable combination of sherry character and nutty spirit.

**Finish** Soft, smooth.

### SCORE 66

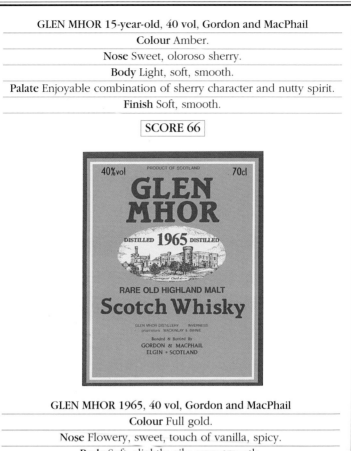

**GLEN MHOR 1965, 40 vol, Gordon and MacPhail**

**Colour** Full gold.

**Nose** Flowery, sweet, touch of vanilla, spicy.

**Body** Soft, slightly oily, very smooth.

**Palate** Very flowery, nutty, vanilla, licorice.

**Finish** Satisfying, soothing, warming, long.

### SCORE 76

**Other versions of Glen Mohr**
A 14-year-old Master of Malt bottling at 43 vol had a very fresh
floweriness in both nose and palate, and a sweetish finish.
SCORE 70. A 1978 at cask strength (63.2 vol) from Gordon and
MacPhail had more fullness and spiciness (especially licorice),
rounded out with sherry. SCORE 77. A 1966 Signatory at 51.6 vol
had more sweetness, licorice and depth of flavours. SCORE 76.

# GLENMORANGIE

**Producer** Macdonald and Muir
**Region** Highlands    **District** Northern Highlands

T HE BIGGEST-SELLING MALT in Scotland, but from a small company. Glenmorangie (the Scots pronounce it to rhyme with "orangey") made an early start: it has been available as a single since the 1920s. It is an easy taste to embrace – a fairly light, sweetish, flowery, spicy malt, in which a French perfume house reported finding 26 fragrances, from almond, bergamot and cinnamon to verbena, vanilla and wild mint.

The water flows through sandstone and is hard. The countryside is rich in heather and clover. Lightly peated malt is used, and a house yeast that imparts an estery, fruity note. The stills are the tallest in Scotland at 5.13 metres (16ft 10¼in) and probably contribute a delicacy to the spirit. A very narrow cut is taken.

The character of the principal version, a 10-year-old, is also shaped by the exclusive use of Bourbon wood in ageing. The same wood is used in the maturation of the single-cask version first released in 1900. This product is rather fussily identified as "The Native Ross-shire Glenmorangie". The distillery, at Tain, is in the county of Ross-shire. All of its whisky is, of course, native to that county.

In the same year, Glenmorangie also introduced an 18-year-old, which in some markets carries a vintage date. This broke ground by spending its last 18 months in sherry casks. In 1993, to celebrate the company's 150th anniversary, a 21-year-old was filled into a stoneware "lemonade" bottle, and there have been older vintages, which sell out very quickly. In 1994, a version of Glenmorangie was released that had been matured in port pipes for two to three years.

Whichever wood is used, the Glenmorangie malts also gain a dimension of character from the coastal location of the distillery. Not only is there the faintest hint of seaweed in the malt, its maturation is also made smoother by the relatively narrow band of temperatures on the coast.

All of Glenmorangie's output is now bottled as a single malt, and the distillery is unusual in that respect. It has been owned since 1918 by Macdonald and Muir, who are also the proprietors of Glen Moray.

**House style** Delicately spicy. In younger ages, an aperitif; in older ages, after dinner.

### GLENMORANGIE 10-year-old, 40 vol

**Colour** Pale gold.

**Nose** Spicy (cinnamon, walnut, sandalwood?), with some flowery sweetness, fresh, a whiff of the sea, enticing.

**Body** On the light side of medium, but with some viscosity.

**Palate** Spicy, flowery and malty-sweet tones that are creamy, almost buttery.

**Finish** Long and rounded.

SCORE 80

### THE NATIVE ROSS-SHIRE GLENMORANGIE 10-year-old, 57.6 vol
(Distilled 10 June 1982, bottled 22 October 1992.)

**Colour** Bright pale gold.

**Nose** Fragrant, salty.

**Body** Medium, smooth.

**Palate** Malty-sweet start, then butterscotch, walnut, sandalwood, sandy-salty notes.

**Finish** Robust, spicy.

SCORE 80

### GLENMORANGIE 18-year-old, 43 vol

**Colour** Full reddish-amber.

**Nose** Sherry, mint, walnuts, sappy, oaky.

**Body** Medium, smooth, fleshier.

**Palate** Sherryish and sweet at first, more walnuts, then the whole pot pourri of spiciness.

**Finish** Aromatic, nutty, lightly oaky.

SCORE 80

**GLENMORANGIE 21-year-old, 43 vol, Sesquicentennial bottling**

**Colour** Deep gold, oily, almost mustardy.

**Nose** Intensely spicy.

**Body** Medium, fleshy.

**Palate** Toffeeish, very satisfying, with walnut, then big development of spices.

**Finish** Juicy oakiness.

SCORE 85

**GLENMORANGIE 1972, 46 vol, Single Barrel Vintage**
(Distilled 2 October 1972, bottled 17 August 1993.)

**Colour** Bright, full gold.

**Nose** Very fresh, flowery, spicy.

**Body** Light to medium, smooth.

**Palate** Smooth, surprisingly light, full of fresh flavours.

**Finish** Spicy, salty, lightly dry, appetising.

SCORE 85

**GLENMORANGIE Port Wood Finish, no age statement, 47 vol**

**Colour** Bronze, with pinkish blush.

**Nose** Pronouncedly fruity and winey.

**Body** Very soft indeed, and smooth.

**Palate** The port seems to bring out the toffeeish notes. It also adds sweeter, winey notes, and melds beautifully with the spiciness of Glenmorangie.

**Finish** Soothing, soporific, relaxing.

SCORE 87

# GLEN MORAY

**Producer** Macdonald and Muir
**Region** Highlands **District** Speyside (Lossie)

I T IS PURELY COINCIDENCE that two malt whiskies with similar names, Glens Morangie and Moray, are made by the two distilleries of the Macdonald and Muir Company. Glen Morangie may be better known, but its more southerly sibling is gaining its own reputation. The principal version of Glen Moray has in recent years been subtitled '93 to mark the year of Macdonald and Muir's foundation a century ago, although the whisky in the bottles is a mere 12 years old. The bottles are packaged in a series of tins, decorated with the liveries of various Highland regiments. There is also a series of vintage-dated bottlings at around 25 years.

It is a second coincidence that both Glenmorangie and Glen Moray were formerly breweries. Moray was converted into a distillery in 1897, acquired by Macdonald and Muir in the 1920s, and extended in 1958.

**House style** Grassy, with barley notes. Aperitif.

**GLEN MORAY 12-year-old, 40 vol**
Perhaps a little austere for some, but elegant and well-balanced.

| | |
|---|---|
| **Colour** Very pale gold. |
| **Nose** Big, rounded, fresh, grassy, new-mown hay, barley notes. |
| **Body** Light, but smooth and firm. |
| **Palate** Ripe, fat barley. |
| **Finish** Fresh, leafy, oatmeal dryness. |

SCORE 75

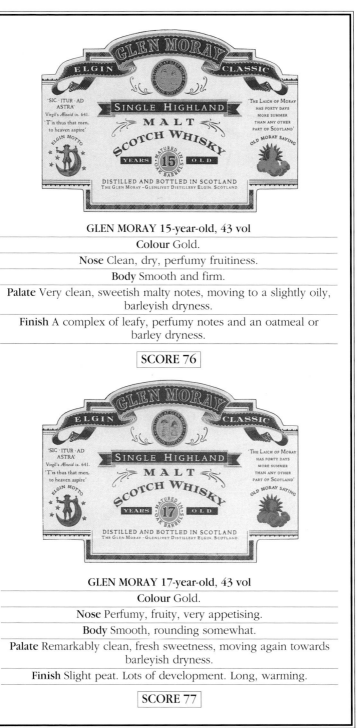

**GLEN MORAY 15-year-old, 43 vol**

**Colour** Gold.

**Nose** Clean, dry, perfumy fruitiness.

**Body** Smooth and firm.

**Palate** Very clean, sweetish malty notes, moving to a slightly oily, barleyish dryness.

**Finish** A complex of leafy, perfumy notes and an oatmeal or barley dryness.

SCORE 76

**GLEN MORAY 17-year-old, 43 vol**

**Colour** Gold.

**Nose** Perfumy, fruity, very appetising.

**Body** Smooth, rounding somewhat.

**Palate** Remarkably clean, fresh sweetness, moving again towards barleyish dryness.

**Finish** Slight peat. Lots of development. Long, warming.

SCORE 77

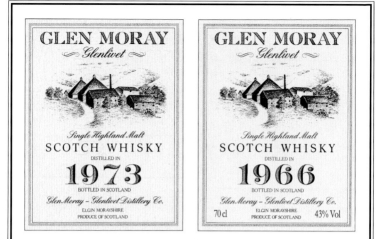

### GLEN MORAY 1973, 43 vol

**Colour** Pale gold, with a tinge of green.

**Nose** Very sweet, but still extremely clean.

**Body** Very smooth indeed.

**Palate** Very complex, with lots of development of sweet (barley, malt and chocolate), delicately spicy notes.

**Finish** Light sweetness and light peatiness. Long and lingering, with surges of flavour.

### SCORE 78

### GLEN MORAY 1966, 43 vol

**Colour** Solid amber.

**Nose** Nutty, juicy, oaky but fresh.

**Body** Smooth, softer.

**Palate** Nutty dryness, malty sweetness and a hint of grassy peatiness, beautifully balanced and rounded. A confident, elegant malt.

**Finish** Sweetness and dryness, with the latter eventually winning. Touches of sappy oakiness. A curiously spicy lift at the very end.

### SCORE 79

### GLEN MORAY 1964, 43 vol

**Colour** Deep gold.

**Nose** Flowery, nutty.

**Body** Smooth, firm.

**Palate** Nutty, rounded, grassy.

**Finish** Spicy, dry, some sappiness.

### SCORE 78

# GLEN ORD

**Producer** United Distillers
**Region** Highlands **District** Northern Highlands

AN IMPORTANT COMPONENT of the Dewar's blends, and an underrated malt as a single. It has impeded its reputation by constantly changing its name. The distillery itself has variously been identified as Muir of Ord, Glen Ord, or simply Ord. In official bottlings, the single malt was for a time known as Glenordie. It has now reverted to Glen Ord. Never mind that the distillery is hardly in a glen; no malt lover would wish to encourage any further changes of identity. As compared with the most recent Glenordie, the new Glen Ord has slightly more sherry character.

The distillery is at the village called Muir of Ord, on the neck of the Black Isle, not far from Inverness. The "Isle" is noted for the cultivation of barley for malting. The distillery has its own maltings, with its open-sided peat-barns. It was founded in 1838 and modernised in 1966.

**House style** Flavoursome, rounded. After dinner.

### GLEN ORD 12-year-old, 40 vol

**Colour** Amber.

**Nose** Rounded, with a dash of sherry, sweet and dry malt notes, and a hint of peatiness.

**Body** Medium to full, soft.

**Palate** Light touch of sherry. Malty and clean all the way through. Begins simply with the taste of malt, then comes a dash of barley-sugar sweetness (and a spicy, gingery note?), followed by a restrained, malty dryness (a hint of peat, too?). Very well-balanced.

**Finish** Dry, gingery, spicy, smooth.

SCORE 75

### GLENORDIE 12-year-old, 40 vol

**Colour** Full, gold.

**Nose** Profound, with sweet and dry malt notes and a hint of peatiness.

**Body** Medium to full, very smooth.

**Palate** Malty, very clean, accented towards sweetness, but with a balancing dryness. So easy to drink, yet full of taste.

**Finish** Dry, gingery, spicy, smooth.

### SCORE 75

### ORD 24-year-old, 46 vol, Cadenhead
A 25-year-old version seems to be very slightly fuller all round.

**Colour** Bronze.

**Nose** Deep and dry, with a hint of peat.

**Body** Medium to full, very smooth.

**Palate** Malty, with a peaty dryness quickly emerging.

**Finish** Peaty, very long, some sherry notes.

### SCORE 77

# GLEN ROTHES

**Producer** Highland Distillers
**Region** Highlands **District** Speyside (Rothes)

**B**LENDERS HAVE ALWAYS prized this malt, but it has never been perceived as a whisky that should be promoted as a single. It is hard to see why. Glen Rothes, or Glenrothes (the name is rendered as one word or two), is a malt full of flavour. Perhaps the blenders' admiration is partly for its performance at the relatively young age of eight. It is remarkably precocious in a sherry-tinged bottling, at this age from Gordon and MacPhail. Being a rich and sweet whisky, it melds beautifully with the sherry. In the 1990s, Glen Rothes got a push from Berry Brothers and Rudd at 12 years old. Now they are concentrating on a 15-year-old version, vintage-dated. The label boasts of delicate peaty undertones, and the whisky delivers them. Has the peat emerged with age, or was the distillery using a more heavily peated malt 15 years ago?

**House style** Perfumy, sweet, spicy-fruity. After dinner.

### GLEN ROTHES 8-year-old, 40 vol, Gordon and MacPhail

**Colour** Full golden to amber.

**Nose** Sweetshop. "Licorice Allsorts".

**Body** Medium to full, syrupy.

**Palate** Round, creamy. Sweetish, with suggestions of raisins, dates and licorice.

**Finish** Licorice. Rooty dryness.

> SCORE 80

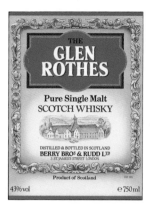

### GLEN ROTHES 12-year-old, 43 vol, Berry Brothers and Rudd

**Colour** Full golden.

**Nose** Some sherry, very soft fruity-spiciness (box of dates? dried apricots? peach skins?) and a hint of perfumy smokiness. Appetising.

**Body** Medium, silky-smooth.

**Palate** Caressing, lightly malty, with the faintest hints of sherry, raisins and licorice. Very complex. Opens up with a dash of water.

**Finish** Spicy, smooth, becoming dry.

### SCORE 81

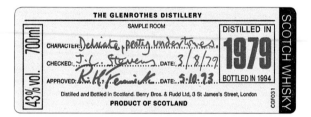

### GLEN ROTHES 1979 (bottled in 1994), 43 vol, Berry Brothers and Rudd

**Colour** solid gold.

**Nose** Delicate peat, as promised on the label.

**Body** Still silky-smooth, but lighter.

**Palate** Licorice. Lots of flavour development. Lots of spiciness. Touches of dried fruit and peat.

**Finish** Spicy, long, dry.

### SCORE 82

# GLEN SCOTIA

**Producer** Gibson International
**Region** Campbeltown

**C**AMPBELTOWN IS TOO EASILY overlooked as a malt region. It still produces extraordinarily distinctive singles from a mere two distilleries. The sea-mist character of the region is at its freshest and most startling in Glen Scotia. The distillery, founded around 1832, is said to be haunted by the ghost of a former proprietor who drowned himself in Campbeltown Loch. After closing in the mid-1980s, the distillery reopened towards the end of that decade. With the Lowland distillery Littlemill, it was backed by the Canadian whisky company, Gibson International. The name was retained after a management buy-out of Littlemill and Glen Scotia.

The whisky, currently available as a single malt, was distilled before the period of closure. Subsequent production is not yet mature. This whisky drinks well when it is young and lively.

**House style** Fresh, salty. Aperitif, or with salty foods.

---

**GLEN SCOTIA 14-year-old, 40 vol**

**Colour** Full, refractive gold.

**Nose** Aromatic, oily, briny, big.

**Body** Seems light as it meets the tongue, but quickly gains dimension, becoming oily and smooth.

**Palate** Dry maltiness, oiliness, saltiness. Very appetite-arousing.

**Finish** Remarkably long and powerful.

SCORE 87

**Other versions of Glen Scotia**
A 12-year-old at 55.8 vol from James MacArthur was smooth and rounded, with a good salty finish. SCORE 86. A 16-year-old at 57.6 vol from Cadenhead was softer, fuller in flavour, saltier and longer. SCORE 88.

# GLEN SPEY

**Producer** IDV/Justerini and Brooks
**Region** Highlands **District** Speyside (Rothes)

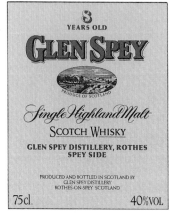

**G**LEN SPEY BELONGS to the same family as the more familiar Knockando, The Singleton of Auchroisk and the lesser-known Strathmill. All are owned by Justerini and Brooks, the "J & B" of blended whisky renown. The original Justerini, from Bologna, Italy, was a distiller and wine merchant. Justerini and Brooks, founded in 1749, is a wine merchant's in St. James's, London. It has for many years been part of the British and worldwide group International Distillers and Vintners (IDV), which also includes the Gilbey's Gin and Smirnoff Vodka brands.

The Glen Spey distillery was founded in 1884 and acquired in 1887 by Gilbey's. Its whisky contributes to blends and has occasionally appeared in some markets as a single malt.

**House style** Light, grassy, nutty. Aperitif.

| GLEN SPEY 8-year-old, 40 vol |
| :---: |
| **Colour** Gold. |
| **Nose** Light, fragrant. |
| **Body** On the light side of medium. |
| **Palate** Aromatic, faint hints of peat, grassiness and nuttiness. |
| **Finish** Light, dryish. |

SCORE 73

# GLENTAUCHERS

**Producer** Allied Distillers
**Region** Highlands    **District** Speyside

HIS DISTILLERY was founded in 1898 and rebuilt in 1965. Its malt has been bottled as a single by various independents, most recently Gordon and MacPhail.

**House style** Dry, medicinal. Aperitif.

### GLENTAUCHERS 1979, 40 vol, Gordon and MacPhail

| |
|---|
| **Colour** Full gold to bronze. |
| **Nose** Touch of sherry, faint phenol. |
| **Body** Light to medium. Smooth. |
| **Palate** Touch of sherry, malty sweetness, fruitiness (raisins and apples?), cloves. |
| **Finish** Dry, clove-like, spicy, eventually a hint of quinine. |

SCORE 72

### GLENTAUCHERS 17-year-old, 46 vol, Cadenhead (distilled 1965, bottled 1982)

| |
|---|
| **Colour** Pale, white wine. |
| **Nose** Light, with both malty and fruity sweetness, or perhaps clove-like, phenolic dryness. |
| **Body** Light but smooth. |
| **Palate** Seems light at first but becomes quite powerful. Malty, but again with its distinctive dryness. |
| **Finish** Very dry, long, warming. |

SCORE 71

# GLENTURRET

**Producer** Highland Distillers
**Region** Highlands **District** Midlands

**A** CLAIMANT TO BEING the oldest distillery in Scotland, Glenturret is without question one of the smallest, producing single malts of a very high quality in a wide range of ages and proofs. There are records of a distillery in the neighbourhood at least as early as 1717, and some of the buildings on the present site date from 1775. The distillery itself was dismantled in the 1920s, then revived in 1959 by a noted whisky enthusiast, James Fairlie. His son, Peter, continues to run the distillery, although it was acquired in 1981 by Cointreau, the French liqueur company. Cointreau subsequently established links with Highland Distilleries. As a result, Glenturret passed to Highland Distilleries in 1990.

The distillery is on the banks of the River Turret, near Crieff in Perthshire. It is tucked away in a steep valley between fields and tree-covered hillsides. In the days of illegal distilling, this would have been a good hiding place. Today it retains its rusticity while also being a tourist attraction.

**House style** Dry, nutty, fresh. Young as an aperitif; older after dinner.

| GLENTURRET 8-year-old, 40 vol |
|---|
| **Colour** Pale, fino sherry. |
| **Nose** Sweet, malty, fresh. |
| **Body** Light and smooth. |
| **Palate** Malty, creamy. |
| **Finish** Surprisingly long, and very lively. |

### SCORE 76

**GLENTURRET 10-year-old, 57.1 vol (100 proof)**

**Colour** Bright, white wine.

**Nose** Very appetising toffeeish maltiness.

**Body** Big, soft.

**Palate** Toffee, roasty notes, very powerful.

**Finish** Nutty, almost juicy.

SCORE 77

**GLENTURRET 12-year-old, 40 vol**

**Colour** Pale gold.

**Nose** Flowery, dry.

**Body** Light to medium. Smooth.

**Palate** Nutty. Dry at first, then malty sweetness and vanilla notes.

**Finish** Sweetness and dryness. Appetising.

SCORE 75

**GLENTURRET 5,000 days old, 40 vol**

**Colour** Full gold.

**Nose** Sweet, with a little more depth.

**Body** Light to medium, smooth.

**Palate** Very tasty. Some raisiny notes, and a good, creamy maltiness.

**Finish** Long.

SCORE 75

**GLENTURRET 15-year-old, 40 vol**
A lovely balance of the components in this luscious malt.

**Colour** Full gold.

**Nose** Profound, with malty and oaky notes.

**Body** Medium, chewy.

**Palate** Malty, roasty, perfumy.

**Finish** Creamy, smooth, glowing.

SCORE 81

### GLENTURRET 15-year-old, 50 vol

**Colour** Full gold.

**Nose** Very flowery, with touches of peat and oak.

**Body** Medium, smooth, becoming chewy.

**Palate** Malty, toasty, nutty, flowery, very perfumy. Some tasters have found elderflower.

**Finish** Smooth, glowing. Very long, with lots of development.

SCORE 82

### GLENTURRET 1972, 43 vol

**Colour** Full gold, with some depth.

**Nose** Profound, with malt, nuttiness and some sherry.

**Body** Medium, rounded.

**Palate** Very complex, with all the components beautifully dovetailed.

**Finish** Nutty, rich, powerful.

SCORE 90

## GLENTURRET 1967, 50 vol

This huge malt is a delight for lovers of heavily sherried whiskies. Given its vintage in combination with its proof, it may well have more intensity of sherry character than any other malt.

**Colour** Deep amber-red.

**Nose** Rich sherry aroma.

**Body** Full, slightly liqueurish, but by no means overbearing.

**Palate** Very sherry-accented.

**Finish** Soft, rich, warming, long.

### SCORE 86

## GLENTURRET 1966, 40 vol

**Colour** Full gold, with a touch of russet.

**Nose** Juicy oak, peat and flowery notes.

**Body** Full, firm, smooth.

**Palate** Very nutty, firm, becoming chewy, but staying just on the sweet side.

**Finish** Dry, oaky, peaty, with late floweriness.

### SCORE 91

# GLENUGIE

**Producer** Whitbread/Long John
**Region** Highlands **District** Eastern Highlands

CONNOISSEURS CHOICE

*Connoisseurs Choice, a range of single malts from various districts of Scotland.*

*In the Highlands are situated the greatest number of malt whisky distilleries.*

SINGLE HIGHLAND
MALT SCOTCH WHISKY
DISTILLED AT
GLENUGIE
DISTILLERY
PROPRIETORS: Long John Distillers Ltd
DISTILLED **1966** DISTILLED

SPECIALLY SELECTED, PRODUCED AND BOTTLED BY
75cl **GORDON & MACPHAIL** 40%vol
ELGIN · SCOTLAND
PRODUCT OF SCOTLAND

**T**HIS ASSERTIVE MALT has never been officially bottled as a single, although it is still available from merchants. It has plenty of character, but the elements are not well-combined or balanced. The supply is finite, since the distillery closed in 1982 and the equipment has been dismantled.

The River Ugie flows into the sea at the port and boat-building town of Peterhead, and the distillery site is nearby, close to the vestiges of an old fishing village. There was first a distillery on the site in the 1830s, but this was converted into a brewery. The present buildings date from 1875. The distillery was last operated by the Whitbread brewing company, at that time under its Long John subsidiary. The distillery buildings still stand, but they have been sold to companies outside the drinks industry.

**House style** Sweet, fruity, medicinal, smoky. Book-at-bedtime.

| GLENUGIE 1966, 40 vol, Connoisseurs Choice |
|:---:|
| **Colour** Bright gold. |
| **Nose** Ripe fruitiness. Fino sherry? Some phenolic smokiness. |
| **Body** Soft, medium, malty, smooth, with some syrupiness. |
| **Palate** Powerful, with honeyish sweetness at first, becoming gingery, with some slightly sulphury sherry notes. Becomes considerably sweeter when water is added. |
| **Finish** Assertive, dry. |

SCORE 70

# GLENURY ROYAL

**Producer** United Distillers
**Region** Highlands   **District** Eastern Highlands

LENURY ROYAL IS ON THE EAST COAST, south of Aberdeen, and close to the fishing port of Stonehaven. The distillery takes its name from the glen that runs through the Ury district. Its founder, Captain Robert Barclay, was a local Member of Parliament and an athlete. He had a friend at court to whom he referred coyly as "Mrs Windsor", and through whose influence he was given permission by King William IV to call his whisky "Royal". The distillery was founded in 1825 and rebuilt in 1966. Its whisky – a good, straightforward Highland malt – can be found as a bottled single malt, although it has never been widely available. It has an uncompromisingly dry, smoky style. Despite its fairly light body, it has plenty of palate. It is a component of the blends made by the small company John Gillon, a subsidiary of Distillers Company Limited until the takeover by United Distillers. The distillery has been mothballed since 1985.

**House style** Aromatic, oily. Aperitif or book-at-bedtime.

| GLENURY ROYAL 12-year-old, 40 vol |
|---|
| **Colour** Bronze. |
| **Nose** Aromatic, dry, smoky. |
| **Body** Light to medium, firm. |
| **Palate** Toasty, dry maltiness, developing towards smokiness. |
| **Finish** Smoky, with a hint of buttery, honeyish sweetness. Very long. |

**SCORE 76**

### GLENURY ROYAL 13-year-old, 46 vol, Cadenhead

**Colour** Pale gold.

**Nose** Sherryish, despite the colour. Dry. Aromatic.

**Body** Light, slightly oily.

**Palate** Sweetish, toasty, becoming dry. Hints of fino sherry?

**Finish** Hints of honey, warming.

### SCORE 75

### GLENURY ROYAL 22-year-old, 46 vol, Cadenhead

**Colour** Amber-red.

**Nose** Sherryish (oloroso?), aromatic, appetising.

**Body** Light to medium, soft.

**Palate** Sherryish start, with lots of oloroso character, developing towards some smokiness.

**Finish** Sherry, smokiness, well-rounded and satisfying.

### SCORE 77

### GLENURY ROYAL 14-year-old, 43 vol, Master of Malt

**Colour** Fino sherry, or even paler.

**Nose** Aromatic, sweetness and sourness.

**Body** Light, oily, smooth.

**Palate** Sweetish, toasty, dry oiliness.

**Finish** Notes of honey and spice.

### SCORE 72

# HIGHLAND PARK

**Producer** Highland Distilleries
**Region** Highlands   **Island** Orkney

**T**HE GREATEST ALL-ROUNDER in the world of malt whisky. Definitely in an island style, but combining all the elements of a classic single malt: smokiness (with its own heather-honey accent); maltiness; smoothness; depth, roundness and fullness of flavour; and length of finish – lovely any time. As a single malt, Highland Park develops to great ages. In blends, it is said to be a catalyst, bringing out the flavours of the other contributing malts.

The distillery is near Kirkwall, capital of the Orkneys. Highland Park, the northernmost of Scotland's distilleries, is said to have been founded in the 1790s. The distillery has its own floor maltings and a well-peated malt is used. The peat is dug locally, from shallow beds that provide a "young", rooty, heathery character. Some maltsters traditionally tried to achieve this character by throwing heather onto the fire.

**House style** Flavoursome and rounded. Restorative or book-at-bedtime.

| HIGHLAND PARK 8-year-old, 40 vol, Gordon and MacPhail |
|---|
| **Colour** Rich gold. |
| **Nose** Smoky and heathery, light. |
| **Body** Medium. |
| **Palate** Fresh, smoky, leafy, sappy, with buttery notes. |
| **Finish** Honeyish, but rather quick. |

**SCORE 85**

**HIGHLAND PARK 8-year-old, 57 vol, Gordon and MacPhail**

Colour Full gold to bronze.

Nose Smoky, heathery, more honeyish.

Body Medium, slightly viscous.

Palate Fresh, smoky, very leafy, very honeyish, buttery.

Finish Honeyish, "cough sweets".

### SCORE 87

A 1983, at 59.7, from Gordon and MacPhail, was similar in character, but richer in sherry and juicy oakiness. SCORE 88.

**HIGHLAND PARK 12-year-old, 40 vol**

Colour Amber.

Nose Smoky, "garden bonfire" sweetness, heathery, malty, hint of sherry.

Body Medium, exceptionally smooth.

Palate Succulent, with smoky dryness, heather-honey sweetness, and maltiness.

Finish Teasing, heathery, delicious.

### SCORE 90

### HIGHLAND PARK 14-year-old, 55.2 vol, Cadenhead

**Colour** Bright, pale gold.

**Nose** Excellent smokiness.

**Body** Medium.

**Palate** Honeyish start, becoming drier, leafy, perfumy.

**Finish** Malty, chewy (like chewing on heather).

### SCORE 87

### HIGHLAND PARK 1972, 54.4 vol, Gordon and MacPhail

**Colour** Fino sherry.

**Nose** Smoky, slightly woody.

**Body** Medium.

**Palate** Dry, heathery, somewhat woody.

**Finish** Perfumy smokiness, a touch woody.

### SCORE 84

### HIGHLAND PARK 24-year-old (1967), 43 vol

**Colour** Amber.

**Nose** Honey, with smooth background smokiness.

**Body** Full.

**Palate** Starts with smooth honey, becoming deeper in flavour, developing to a smooth, perfumy smokiness.

**Finish** Smooth, honeyish, with light fruitiness. Soothing.

### SCORE 93

# IMPERIAL

**Producer** Allied Distillers
**Region** Highlands **District** Speyside

**IMPERIAL**
Built in 1897, the year of
Queen Victoria's Diamond
Jubilee, the Imperial
Distillery stands
majestically among the
dark woods of Carron,
in a fold of the hills
which encompass the
glittering Spey.

Specially selected,
produced and bottled by
and under the
responsibility of
*Gordon & Macphail,*
Elgin, Scotland.
Regd. Bottler.

A POWERFUL, OLD-FASHIONED Highland malt that can be found only in independent bottlings. Gordon and McPhail is now authorised to bottle the whisky as a single malt. Recent bottlings have been as flavoursome as ever, but less peaty. The Imperial distillery is in Carron, just across the river from Dailuaine, with which it was historically linked. It was founded in 1897 and extended in 1965. After a brief closure in the mid-1980s, it was reopened by Allied.

**House style** Big and sweet, liqueurish. After dinner or at bedtime.

---

**IMPERIAL 1979, 40 vol, Gordon and MacPhail**

**Colour** Full gold, with an amber tinge.

**Nose** Some peaty oiliness.

**Body** Medium to full, soft.

**Palate** Sherry, juicy oak and vanilla at first, developing to an intense, spicy sweetness and malty cereal-grain notes. A complex of lively, distinct flavours.

**Finish** Sweet, lively, intense.

SCORE 76

**Other versions of Imperial**
A 14-year-old at 64.9 vol from Cadenhead was less sherried but still very sweet in its maltiness, with a touch of heather and peat. SCORE 76.

# INCHGOWER

**Producer** United Distillers
**Region** Highlands  **District** Speyside

SPEYSIDE
SINGLE MALT
*SCOTCH WHISKY*

The *Oyster Catcher* is a common *sight*
around the

**INCHGOWER**

*distillery*, which stands *close* to the *sea*
on the mouth of the *RIVER SPEY*
near *BUCKIE*. *Inchgower*,
established in 1824, produces *one* of the
most *distinctive single* malt whiskies
in *SPEYSIDE*. It is a malt for the
*discerning drinker* ~ a *complex* aroma
precedes a *fruity, spicy*
taste *//* with a hint of *salt*.

AGED **14** YEARS

43% vol    70cl

Distilled & Bottled in SCOTLAND.
INCHGOWER DISTILLERS,
Buckie, Banffshire, Scotland

**I**NCHGOWER LIES NEAR the fishing town of Buckie, and its whisky is less of a Speyside malt in character than a coastal one. To the palate expecting a more flowery, elegant Speyside malt, this one can seem assertive, or even astringent, in its saltiness. With familiarity, that can become addictive. A lovely, sustaining dram after a stroll by the sea or a day's fishing. An earlier 12-year-old was slightly sweeter and fractionally more sherryish than the newer 14-year-old, which has more distillery character. The Inchgower distillery was built in 1871, and expanded in 1966.

**House style** Dry, salty. Restorative or aperitif.

---

### INCHGOWER 14-year-old, 43 vol, Flora and Fauna

**Colour** Pale gold.

**Nose** An almost chocolatey spiciness, then sweet notes like edible seaweed and finally a whiff of saltier sea character. Overall, dry and complex.

**Body** Light to medium. Smooth.

**Palate** Starts sweet and malty, with lots of flavour developing, eventually becoming drier and salty.

**Finish** Very salty, lingering appetisingly on the tongue.

### SCORE 76

# INCHMURRIN

**Producer** William Morton
**Region** Highlands **District** Western Highlands

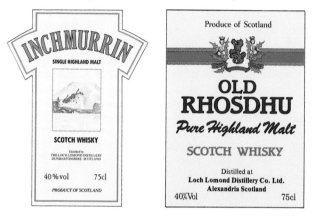

**I**NCHMURRIN IS A MONASTIC ISLAND in Loch Lomond. Just south of the loch, the single malt of the same name is made. The distillery is called Loch Lomond, and it produces another malt called Old Rhosdhu. Loch Lomond can make more than one malt because its pot-stills are of an unusual design, and can produce whiskies of different weights.

**House style** Medicinal. Restorative.

### INCHMURRIN, no age statement, 40 vol

| | |
|---|---|
| **Colour** Full amber (darker than the 12-year-old version). | |

**Nose** Eucalyptus?

**Body** Medium.

**Palate** Smooth, pleasantly oily. Very long flavour development. Eucalyptus. Very unusual.

**Finish** Soothing, warming. After a dip in Loch Lomond?

**SCORE 67**

### OLD RHOSDHU, no age statement, 40 vol

**Colour** Amber.

**Nose** Scented. A luxurious malt to drink in the bath?

**Body** Light.

**Palate** Dry, perfumy, spicy.

**Finish** Wintergreen? Perhaps not the bath – the sauna.

**SCORE 65**

# INVERLEVEN

**Producer** Allied Distillers
**Region** Lowlands   **District** Western Lowlands

**A** VERY RARE MALT, produced in the imposing distillery complex at Ballantine's home-base in Dumbarton. For many years, this complex operated two pot-still houses to produce malt whisky for the Ballantine blends. Each produced a different malt whisky, and the two were known internally as Inverleven and Lomond. Neither malt has ever been officially released as a single, but Inverleven can be found in independent bottlings. Recently, the Inverleven stills have been de-commissioned, and all the malt that is produced at Dumbarton comes from the Lomond system. This system generally produces a heavier, oilier spirit. In addition to these whiskies, a very wide range of other malts go into the soft but complex Ballantine blends. Further bottlings of Inverleven are expected from Gordon and MacPhail.

**House style** Perfumy, fruity, oily. With nuts at Christmas.

*The edifice of the Ballantine's cluster of distilleries towers above the River Leven, which gives its name to a rare malt.*

### INVERLEVEN 17-year-old, 46 vol, Cadenhead
### (Distilled 1966, Bottled 1984)

**Colour** Gold.

**Nose** Dry, delicate, perfumy, grassy, a hint of smoke, cedarwood, nectarine?

**Body** Seems light at first, but becomes fuller and rounder.

**Palate** Gingery, crisp.

**Finish** Fruity and powerful.

SCORE 67

### INVERLEVEN 1979, 40 vol, Gordon and MacPhail

**Colour** A good medium amber.

**Nose** Sherried, perfumy, grassy, faint hint of peat-smoke.

**Body** Medium, soft.

**Palate** Oily, cedarwood, grass.

**Finish** Waxy, fruity. Very restrained orange-skin. Long. Warming.

SCORE 71

### INVERLEVEN 21-year-old, 46 vol, Cadenhead

**Colour** Pale greeny-gold.

**Nose** Perfumy, grassy, with a hint of nectarine?

**Body** Seems light at first but very well-rounded.

**Palate** Orangey, gingery.

**Finish** Expressive, orangey, appetising.

SCORE 69

# JURA

**Producer** Invergordon
**Region** Highlands   **Island** Jura

IN THE INNER HEBRIDES, close to Islay, lies the isle of Jura, inhabited by 225 people (George Orwell was briefly a resident) and rather more deer. It is also noted for two mountain peaks known as the Paps (breasts) of Jura, and one malt distillery.

The distillery seems to have been founded around 1810, and was rebuilt in 1876. Although a couple of buildings dating back to its early days are still in use, the present distillery was built during the late 1950s and early 1960s, and enlarged in the 1970s. It was owned for a time by Scottish and Newcastle Breweries, and its malt whisky is an important component of the Mackinlay blends.

Lightly peated malt is used, and the water flows primarily over rock. The stills have very high necks, producing a light, relatively clean spirit, with only a slight island character.

**House style** Piney, lightly oily, soft, salty. Aperitif.

*The famous Paps, or mountains, of the island of Jura seen from across the Sound of Islay.*

### ISLE OF JURA 10-year-old, 40 vol

**Colour** Golden.

**Nose** Oily, lightly piney, earthy, salty, dry.

**Body** Light, slightly oily, soft.

**Palate** Sweetish, malty, oily, slowly developing a slight island dryness and saltiness.

**Finish** A little malty sweetness and some saltiness.

**SCORE 71**

### ISLE OF JURA 10-year-old, 63.9 vol, Cadenhead

**Colour** White wine.

**Nose** Fragrant, some peatiness, floweriness and saltiness.

**Body** Light and soft.

**Palate** Malty sweetness, oily and flowery.

**Finish** Sweet, then a surge of flowery and salty flavours.

**SCORE 71**

**ISLE OF JURA 20-year-old, 54 vol, (cask strength)
limited edition**

**Colour** Golden.

**Nose** Creamy, oily, dryish.

**Body** More round.

**Palate** Flavours more tightly combined, but slowly revealing
themselves. Flowery, sweet, piney, earthy.

**Finish** Intensely salty and satisfying.

SCORE 78

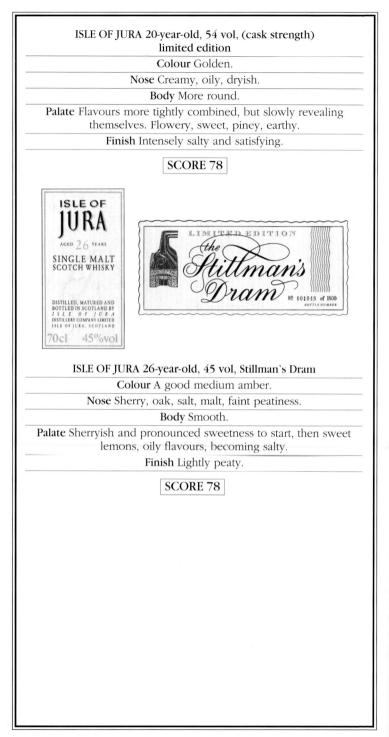

**ISLE OF JURA 26-year-old, 45 vol, Stillman's Dram**

**Colour** A good medium amber.

**Nose** Sherry, oak, salt, malt, faint peatiness.

**Body** Smooth.

**Palate** Sherryish and pronounced sweetness to start, then sweet
lemons, oily flavours, becoming salty.

**Finish** Lightly peaty.

SCORE 78

# KINCLAITH

**Producer** Whitbread/Long John
**Region** Lowlands    **District** Western Lowlands

**T**HERE WAS ONCE quite a scatter of malt distilleries in Glasgow, and there have been about half a dozen this century. Kinclaith was the last. It was built in 1957 as part of the complex already housing the Strathclyde grain distillery. The original owner was the American company Schenley, through its subsidiaries Seager Evans and Long John. When the latter was sold to Whitbread in 1975, Kinclaith was dismantled. The independent bottlers still have stocks of Kinclaith. Gordon and MacPhail bottlings reveal a soft, seductive malt, perhaps helped along by a little sherry; the Cadenhead version is much drier.

**House style** Light, melony. Aperitif.

KINCLAITH 1967, 40 vol, Connoisseurs Choice

| Colour Amber. |
| --- |
| **Nose** Smoky, some sherry, faintly sulphury. |
| **Body** Light, delicate. |
| **Palate** Light, soft, restrained fruitiness. Melon? |
| **Finish** Soothing, tasty. Melon. Sherry. |

SCORE 68

**KINCLAITH 20-year-old, 46 vol, Cadenhead**

**Colour** Very pale.

**Nose** Smoky, phenolic.

**Body** Light and soft.

**Palate** Light, gingery. A light, aromatic, aperitif dryness.

**Finish** Light, dry.

SCORE 65

**KINCLAITH 1966, 40 vol, Connoisseurs Choice**

**Colour** Bronze.

**Nose** Smoky.

**Body** Light, very soft.

**Palate** Lightly fruity (melon dusted with ginger?).

**Finish** Soft, tasty, melon-like.

SCORE 69

# KNOCKANDO

**Producer** IDV/Justerini and Brooks
**Region** Highlands   **District** Speyside

**K**NOCKANDO IS THE FLAGSHIP distillery of IDV/Justerini and Brooks, and produces a malt whisky of some elegance. It is marketed as a single malt under its season of distillation; the year of bottling is also indicated on the label. The notion is that the whisky is bottled when it is mature, rather than at a specific age. The age range of principal vintages offered varies between 10 and 15 years. The aim is to produce a consistently mature malt so that one vintage does not differ dramatically from another, but there may be differences in the degree of floweriness, maltiness or sweetness. An older range has been offered as Special Selection and a more mature bottling as Extra Old Reserve.

The distillery's name translates as "a little black hill". Its water rises from granite and flows over peat. Knockando was established in 1898 and much of the building is original.

**House style** Elegant, with suggestions of berry fruits. Aperitif.

### KNOCKANDO 1978 (bottled 1993), 43 vol

| |
|---|
| **Colour** Pale gold. |
| **Nose** Fragrant, perfumy. Soft. Raspberries in cream. |
| **Body** Light, but notably smooth. Lightly creamy. |
| **Palate** Soft, creamy, fresh. Restrained fruit. Slightly liqueurish. |
| **Finish** Soft. Light cream and toffee. Touch of sherry. Becoming drier as it slowly and gently fades. |

### SCORE 76

**KNOCKANDO Special Selection, 1976 (bottled 1992), 43 vol**

**Colour** Pale to medium gold.

**Nose** Fractionally more raspberry and sherry, and a faint hint of peat.

**Body** Soft, creamy.

**Palate** Emphatically more raspberry character. Drier, with a faint hint of peat.

**Finish** Very appetising.

**SCORE 77**

**KNOCKANDO Extra Old Reserve, 1968 (bottled 1992), 43 vol**

**Colour** Medium to full gold.

**Nose** Surprisingly assertive, with oak, sherry and fruit.

**Body** Light to medium.

**Palate** Raspberries, strawberries, cream, sherry and oak. Still a soft, mellow, elegant whisky, but with greater depth.

**Finish** A hint of peat, fruit, and a touch of oak.

**SCORE 79**

# LADYBURN

**Producer** William Grant and Sons
**Region** Lowlands   **District** Western Lowlands

PURE MALT SCOTCH WHISKY
from
*LADYBURN*
**Distillery**

Proprietors: William Grant & Sons Ltd.

Bottled by Wm. Cadenhead,
**75 cl**    18 Golden Square, Aberdeen    **46% vol**
Scotland

O NCE GLENFIDDICH'S LOWLAND partner and likewise a component of the Grant's blended whiskies. Unlike Glenfiddich, however, Ladyburn was never perceived by its owners as a whisky for consumption as a single malt. It has a certain fresh-faced charm, but no pretensions to depth of character. Ladyburn was opened in quite recent times, in 1966, alongside the company's Girvan grain distillery. It then closed in the mid-1970s, although Girvan remains open. The company still has stocks of the Ladyburn whisky, but little of it appears as a single malt, and then from independent bottlers.

**House style** Perfumy and dry. Aperitif.

| LADYBURN 20-year-old, 46 vol, Cadenhead |
| :---: |
| **Colour** Very pale, white wine. |
| **Nose** Light, fruity, dry. |
| **Body** Light and soft. |
| **Palate** Light, medium-sweet, quickly becoming perfumy and dry. |
| **Finish** Powerful, dry. |

### SCORE 57

# LAGAVULIN

**Producer** United Distillers
**Region** Islay   **District** South shore

T HE CLASSIC ISLAY WHISKY, with the driest start of any single malt. More instantly assertive even than its neighbours, Ardbeg and Laphroaig, it also has a more sustained power and a greater complexity. Intensely dry, from its pungent bouquet to its astonishing long finish.

Its attack is reminiscent of Lapsang Souchong tea, but supported by a big, malty, sweetish (Darjeeling this time?) background. The third generous element is sherry. A big, immensely sophisticated whisky. Some devotees feel that the dryness is better expressed in the 12-year-old, which was the principal version until largely replaced by the 16-year-old. Others feel that the greater sherry character of the 16-year-old makes for a more complete symphony.

*Decanter* magazine compared the relationship of Lagavulin and Laphroaig on Islay with that of Cheval Blanc and Petrus in Bordeaux. In name at least, Lagavulin must be the Cheval Blanc, as it contributes malt whisky to the White Horse blends, and the animal decorates the distillery sign. The distillery's water arrives by way of a fast-flowing stream that no doubt picks up plenty of peat on the way there. The maturation warehouses are battered by the sea, and they have their own jetty.

Lagavulin (pronounced "lagga-voolin") means "the hollow where the mill is". There are reputed to have been ten illicit stills on this bay in the mid-1700s. There were two distilleries here in the early 1800s, and they combined in the 1830s.

**House style** Dry, smoky, complex. Restorative or nightcap.

*When the seas are high, Lagavulin's outer walls are knee-high in salt water.*

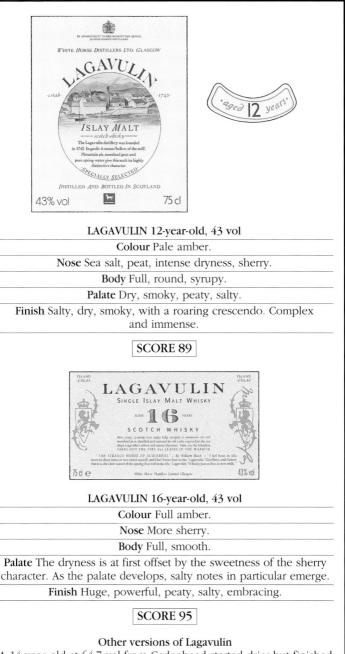

### LAGAVULIN 12-year-old, 43 vol

**Colour** Pale amber.

**Nose** Sea salt, peat, intense dryness, sherry.

**Body** Full, round, syrupy.

**Palate** Dry, smoky, peaty, salty.

**Finish** Salty, dry, smoky, with a roaring crescendo. Complex and immense.

### SCORE 89

### LAGAVULIN 16-year-old, 43 vol

**Colour** Full amber.

**Nose** More sherry.

**Body** Full, smooth.

**Palate** The dryness is at first offset by the sweetness of the sherry character. As the palate develops, salty notes in particular emerge.

**Finish** Huge, powerful, peaty, salty, embracing.

### SCORE 95

### Other versions of Lagavulin
A 14-year-old at 64.7 vol from Cadenhead started drier but finished sweeter and was less complex. SCORE 88. Another Cadenhead at 15 years old and 64.4 vol was lighter but saltier. SCORE 87.

# LAPHROAIG

**Producer** Allied Distillers
**Region** Islay   **District** South shore

**L**OVE IT OR HATE IT, Laphroaig's distinctiveness is too much for even some hardened malt-lovers. The medicinal character is addictive to some devotees, but an impenetrable barrier to the faint-hearted. Like hospital gauze, said one taster. Medicinal, reminiscent of mouthwash or disinfectant, phenolic, tar-like? That is the whole point: the iodine-like, seaweed character of Islay. The famous Laphroaig attack has diminished a little in recent years, unmasking more of the sweetness of the malt, but it is still a very characterful whisky, with a distinctively oily body.

Laphroaig has its own peat-beds on Islay, and a beautifully maintained floor maltings at the distillery. Its maturation warehouses face directly onto the sea. The distillery was built in the 1820s by the Johnston family, whose name is still on the label. In 1847 the founder died after falling into a vat of partially made whisky. There were, no doubt, more raised eyebrows when, in the late 1950s and early 1960s, the distillery was owned by a woman, Miss Bessie Williamson.

**House style** Medicinal. Nightcap.

LAPHROAIG®

**SINGLE ISLAY MALT
SCOTCH WHISKY**

**10**
*Years Old*

**The most richly flavoured of
all Scotch whiskies**

ESTABLISHED
**1815**

DISTILLED AND BOTTLED IN SCOTLAND BY

D. JOHNSTON & CO., (LAPHROAIG), LAPHROAIG DISTILLERY, ISLE OF ISLAY.

70cl e                          43%vol

---

**LAPHROAIG 10-year-old, 43 vol**

**Colour** Full, refractive, gold.

**Nose** Medicinal, phenolic, seaweedy, with a hint of sherry.

**Body** Medium, oily.

**Palate** Seaweedy, salty, oily.

**Finish** Round and very dry.

**SCORE 86**

**LAPHROAIG®**

AGED **15** YEARS

**SINGLE *ISLAY* MALT**
**SCOTCH WHISKY**

"The most richly flavoured of all Scotch Whiskies"

EST'D **1815** EST'D

DISTILLED AND BOTTLED IN SCOTLAND BY
D.JOHNSTON & CO .,(LAPHROAIG), LAPHROAIG DISTILLERY, ISLE OF ISLAY

**750 ml**     PRODUCT OF SCOTLAND **43%** ALC/VOL

L00107                                                    L00108

### LAPHROAIG 15-year-old, 43 vol

**Colour** Pale amber.

**Nose** Drier, deeper.

**Body** Medium to full, with a soothing oiliness.

**Palate** A deceptive moment of sherryish sweetness, then a burst of Islay intensity.

**Finish** Round, dry, long, warming.

### SCORE 89

### LAPHROAIG 16-year-old, 57 vol, Cadenhead

**Colour** Pale gold.

**Nose** Very dry, with a faint hint of sherry.

**Body** Full, very oily.

**Palate** Powerful, sweet at first, then salty and dry.

**Finish** Oily, salty, warming.

### SCORE 81

### LAPHROAIG 1974, 55 vol, Signatory

**Colour** Deep amber-red, almost tawny.

**Nose** Intense seaweed. Slightly sour.

**Body** Medium to full, drying on the tongue.

**Palate** Intense, sweet, sherry, edible seaweed, phenolic. High points for character, but lacks balance.

**Finish** Dry, very late seaweed, warming.

### SCORE 87

# LINKWOOD

**Producer** United Distillers
**Region** Highlands   **District** Speyside (Lossie)

**R**OMANTIC TASTING NOTES are evoked by this perfumy, malty Speyside classic. It has an elegance and complexity beloved of devotees, although it never hit the heights of fashion. This malt has traditionally been bottled with a definite sherry accent. The sherry ageing seemed to complement the perfumy sweetness of the whisky. A new version has no obvious sherry character, so that the whisky itself shines through. The new version, in United Distillers Flora and Fauna series, is arguably more assertively characterful, but less complete.

Linkwood is on the Lossie, close to Elgin. It was founded in the 1820s and, despite its growth, it has a traditionalist outlook. Whisky-writer Philip Morrice recalls that at one stage the management forbade the removal of spiders' webs in case a change in the environment should affect the whisky.

**House style** Floral. Rose water? Violets? Delicious with a
slice of fruit cake.

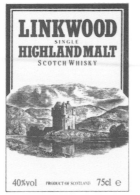

| LINKWOOD 12-year-old, 40 vol |
| --- |
| **Colour** Full, gold. |
| **Nose** Sweet, light-but-definite sherry character, and some depth. |
| **Body** Medium, rounded. |
| **Palate** Sweet start, developing to lightly smoky dryness. |
| **Finish** Dryish, smooth, confident, lots of finesse. |

**SCORE 83**

## LINKWOOD 12-year-old, 43 vol, Flora and Fauna

**Colour** Very pale, white wine.

**Nose** Remarkably flowery. The rose water without the sherry. Fragrant. Clean and sweet.

**Body** Medium, rounded, slightly syrupy.

**Palate** Starts slowly, and has a long sustained development to its full, rosy, fresh sweetness. One to savour.

**Finish** Perfumy, faintly smoky, long.

### SCORE 82

## LINKWOOD 14-year-old, 58.5 vol, Cadenhead

**Colour** Chestnut.

**Nose** Very oaky, oily, sherryish.

**Body** Medium, smooth, then drying on the tongue.

**Palate** Oaky, sappy, sherryish, almonds, marzipan, violets.

**Finish** Oaky, sappy, sherryish, spicy.

### SCORE 83

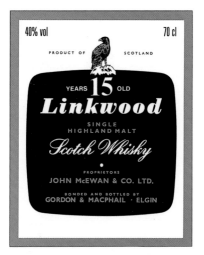

**LINKWOOD 15-year-old, 40 vol, Gordon and MacPhail**

**Colour** Full gold to amber.

**Nose** Intensely floral. Roses, violets.

**Body** Medium, falling away slightly.

**Palate** Floral. Roses, violets, almonds, marzipan.

**Finish** Light oakiness, drying out slightly.

SCORE 84

# LITTLEMILL

**Producer** Gibson International
**Region** Lowlands  **District** Western Lowlands

**A** CLASSIC LOWLAND MALT from a distillery that may be the oldest in Scotland. Among several claimants to the greatest antiquity, Littlemill cites the earliest specific date for its foundation: 1772. The first clear records of its ownership, however, date from 1817. It was rebuilt in 1875, although its overgrown, cottage-like buildings look older. Triple-distillation was used until the 1930s.

The site, at Bowling, is between Glasgow and Dumbarton. The Lowland style is to produce single malts that are light in taste, gentle, soft, sweet and fresh. Littlemill's is a whole-hearted example. The full freshness is best experienced in the 8-year-old official bottling. Older versions in independent bottlings tend to be rounder and firmer.

**House style** Marshmallow soft. A restorative, or perhaps with dessert.

### LITTLEMILL 8-year-old, 43 vol

| | |
|---|---|
| **Colour** | Very pale, white wine. |
| **Nose** | Marshmallow? Perhaps toasted marshmallows. |
| **Body** | Light to medium, soft. |
| **Palate** | Deliciously malty-sweet, yet somehow not overbearing. Marshmallow again, perhaps powdery icing sugar? |
| **Finish** | Very smooth, slight dryness. Coconut? |

### SCORE 83

PRODUCT OF SCOTLAND

SINGLE MALT SCOTCH WHISKY
from

# LITTLEMILL
## Distillery

Proprietors: Littlemill Distillery Co. Ltd.

Bottled by Wm. Cadenhead,
18 Golden Square, Aberdeen
Scotland

75 cl          46% vol

**LITTLEMILL 22-year-old, 46 vol, Cadenhead**

**Colour** Pale gold.

**Nose** Drier, deeper, more aromatic.

**Body** Light to medium, well-rounded.

**Palate** Sweet but beautifully rounded.

**Finish** Oily, coconut-like.

## SCORE 83

# LOCHNAGAR

**Producer** United Distillers
**Region** Highlands   **District** Eastern Highlands

Q UEEN VICTORIA IS REPUTED to have enjoyed this malt and to have used it to lace her claret, thereby ruining two of the world's greatest drinks. She visited the distillery, which is at the foot of the mountain of Lochnagar and close to the Royal family's Scottish home at Balmoral.

A man believed originally to have been an illicit whisky-maker established the first legal Lochnagar distillery in 1826, and the present premises were built in 1845. Three years later, the Royal family acquired Balmoral. The then owner recorded that he wrote a note inviting Prince Albert to come and visit, and was rewarded accordingly the very next day. Soon afterwards, the distillery began to supply the Queen, and became known as Royal Lochnagar. Over the years, the distillery has been rebuilt three times, most recently in 1967. It still has the look of a farmhouse, with its small museum and coffee shop in former cowsheds.

The water flows from the small peak of Lochnagar over peat and heather. The stills are shaped like up-turned wine glasses and the copper pipework is endless and gleaming. The 12-year-old is aged in second-fill casks, while the Selected Reserve has 50 per cent sherry.

**House style** Malty, fruity, spicy, cake-like. After dinner.

*With its "Royal" prefix restored and the release of its Selected Reserve Malt, this is becoming a justifiably better-known distillery.*

### ROYAL LOCHNAGAR 12-year-old, 43 vol

**Colour** Full, gold.

**Nose** Big, with some smokiness.

**Body** Medium to full. Smooth.

**Palate** Light smokiness, restrained fruitiness and malty sweetness.

**Finish** Again, dry smokiness and malty sweetness. The first impression is of dryness, then comes the sweet, malty counterpoint.

### SCORE 80

### ROYAL LOCHNAGAR Selected Reserve, no age statement, 43 vol

**Colour** Amber-red.

**Nose** Lots of sherry. Spices, ginger cake.

**Body** Big, smooth.

**Palate** Lots of sherry, malty sweetness, spiced bread, ginger cake.

**Finish** Smoky.

### SCORE 83

# LOCHSIDE

Producer Macnab Distilleries
**Region** Highlands    **District** Eastern Highlands

O NCE THE FAMOUS James Deuchar brewery, Lochside, in Montrose, has been a distillery since 1957. Since 1973 the distillery has been under Spanish ownership, and much of its malt goes into the Distilieras y Crienza blended whisky, a major product in Spain. The distillery has been mothballed since 1992.

**House style** Fruity, dry, gentle. Aperitif.

### LOCHSIDE 10-year-old, 40 vol

| |
|---|
| **Colour** Gold. |
| **Nose** Some flowering currant. |
| **Body** Light to medium, soft, smooth. |
| **Palate** Malty start, but not especially sweet. Lots of flavour development. Fruity (blackcurrant?). Becoming dry. |
| **Finish** Gentle, not very long. |

### SCORE 74

**Other versions of Lochside**
A Gordon and MacPhail 1966 at 40 vol was sherryish with a sweet finish. SCORE 73. The Signatory 1966 at 43 vol was drier and slightly oaky. SCORE 71. A Signatory 1959 at 58.5 vol was sherryish and oaky. SCORE 72.

# LONGMORN

**Producer** Seagram/Chivas
**Region** Highlands   **District** Speyside (Lossie)

ONE OF THE GREATEST Speyside malts, cherished by connoisseurs but not widely known. Longmorn is admired for its complexity, its combination of smoothness and fullness of character, and from its big bouquet to its long finish. It is noted for its cereal-grain maltiness and oily flavours, reminiscent of beeswax.

Longmorn was built in 1894–95, and has a disused waterwheel and a workable steam engine. It was extended twice during the 1970s.

In recent years, the company has begun to market the Longmorn whisky more actively as a 15-year-old. It is to be hoped that this does not result in it eventually being produced faster and with a blander character.

**House style** Tongue-coating, oily, malty. Versatile, delightful before dinner and especially good with dessert.

### LONGMORN 12-year-old, 40 vol

**Colour** Full, bright, gold.

**Nose** Complex, firm.

**Body** Firm, smooth, gentle.

**Palate** Deliciously fresh, cereal-grain maltiness. Slow, long flavour development, evolving towards a clean, flowery fruitiness.

**Finish** Clean, smooth, appetising. Surely a pre-dinner malt.

**SCORE 85**

LONGMORN 15-year-old, 43 vol

| | |
|---|---|
| **Colour** | Full, gold. |
| **Nose** | Big, slightly oily, barley malt, flowery notes. |
| **Body** | Smooth, rounded, medium to big. |
| **Palate** | Very emphatic, fresh, clean, cereal-grain maltiness. |
| **Finish** | Clean, malty but dry, nutty, hint of sherry, appetising, very long. |

SCORE 87

LONGMORN 19-year-old, 45 vol, Cadenhead

| | |
|---|---|
| **Colour** | Gold to full gold. |
| **Nose** | Cereal grain, malt, smoke. |
| **Body** | Smooth, rounded, big. |
| **Palate** | Beeswax, oiliness, cereal grain, malty, smoky. |
| **Finish** | Some malty sweetness and perfumy notes. |

SCORE 88

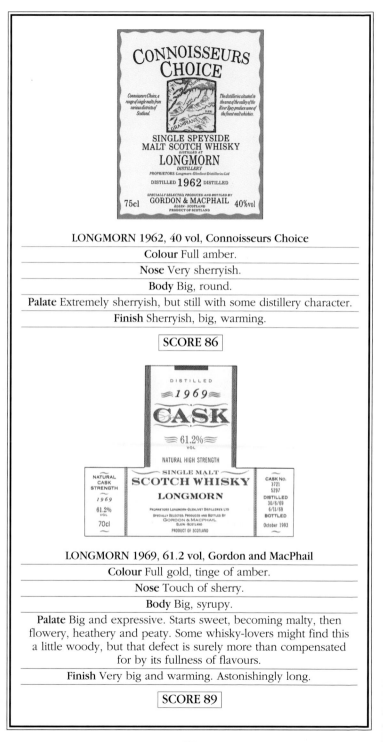

**LONGMORN 1962, 40 vol, Connoisseurs Choice**

**Colour** Full amber.

**Nose** Very sherryish.

**Body** Big, round.

**Palate** Extremely sherryish, but still with some distillery character.

**Finish** Sherryish, big, warming.

SCORE 86

**LONGMORN 1969, 61.2 vol, Gordon and MacPhail**

**Colour** Full gold, tinge of amber.

**Nose** Touch of sherry.

**Body** Big, syrupy.

**Palate** Big and expressive. Starts sweet, becoming malty, then flowery, heathery and peaty. Some whisky-lovers might find this a little woody, but that defect is surely more than compensated for by its fullness of flavours.

**Finish** Very big and warming. Astonishingly long.

SCORE 89

# THE MACALLAN

**Producer** Macallan
**Region** Highlands    **District** Speyside

"T HE ROLLS ROYCE OF SINGLE MALTS" is a soubriquet often bestowed upon The Macallan. From its efforts to secure Golden Promise barley and its insistence upon small stills (it builds more, rather than making them bigger) to its love affair with sherry ageing (always in dry oloroso casks, shipped unbroken from Spain), Macallan has a clear view of its standards. In the big, heavily sherried style, there is no malt more widely acknowledged than The Macallan. It is the classic example of this type of Speyside whisky.

The sherry ageing, and its consistency, are the trademark of The Macallan. Sceptics argue that the sherry dominates, but that is manifestly not true. There are more heavily sherried whiskies, but none with the particular profile of The Macallan: a complex of sherry, maltiness, slight smokiness, flowering currant and Calvados-like notes, with its own distinctive dryness, roundness and depth. It is a malt with big, bold, clear tones from aroma to finish. Between those two extremes is a beautifully composed whole.

Even the 7-year-old malt, bottled exclusively for the Italian market, is full of flavour. One of The Macallan's celebrated adherents, novelist Kingsley Amis, insists that the 10-year-old version is "the best glass". There is considerable development of character between the 10- and the 12-year-old, while many devotees prefer the 18-year-old. The whisky-writer Wallace Milroy proposed the 1964 vintage as the stuff of legend. A rival case, so to speak, might be made for the 1950, with its slightly oily, peaty palate and spectacularly long finish. There have been a number of special editions. In 1993, a 60-year-old was bought for £6,400 by a bar manager in Osaka, Japan.

There has probably been whisky made on the Macallan site, on a small hill overlooking the Spey near Craigellachie, since the late 1700s. A farmer on the hillside first made whisky there from his own barley. A manor house from this period has been restored as a venue for entertaining private guests. An illustration of the house is used on the box that accommodates each bottle of The Macallan. It is intended to convey the sense of a whisky "Château", and perhaps to offset the harder lines of what is a functional-looking distillery.

The first licenced distillation at Macallan is said to have taken place in the earliest days of legalised production, in 1824. In 1892, the business passed into the hands of the family who still manage Macallan and have a major share in the company. Macallan went public in the 1960s and was thus able to finance the laying down of large stocks of whisky for maturation, and a decade of expansion. Each extension involved the building of a new still-house, so that the company could increase production without altering the size of its stills.

The company was already renowned among blenders, who use its malt whisky as a top dressing, but in the 1960s Macallan was available as a bottled single malt only on Speyside. Although the larger share of the malt continues to be reserved for blending, a new generation of family management decided to market a bottled single; The Macallan was launched in Britain in 1980. Like other pioneers of singles, Macallan has tried to limit independent bottlings. There is, nonetheless, a well-known example, quaintly labelled "As We Get It", and marketed by J. G. Thomson, the spirits and wine subsidiary of Bass in Scotland.

**House style** Big-bodied, oaky, sherryish, flowery.
After dinner.

**THE MACALLAN 7-year-old, 40 vol**
(Italian market only.)

| |
|---|
| **Colour** Bright amber. |
| **Nose** Sherry, with dry maltiness in the background. |
| **Body** Medium to full. |
| **Palate** Sherryish and sweetish, with malt and fruit coming up behind. |
| **Finish** Satisfying, sherryish, malty-buttery. A light digestif. |

### SCORE 81

### THE MACALLAN 10-year-old, 40 vol

**Colour** Amber.

**Nose** Sherry and buttery, honeyish, malt character. Lots of roundness and depth, even at this young age.

**Body** Full, without being syrupy.

**Palate** Lots of sherry, without being rich. Plenty of malt. Sweetish.

**Finish** Satisfying, malty, gingery, becoming dry, with a hint of smoke.

### SCORE 87

### THE MACALLAN 10-year-old, 57 vol (100 proof)

**Colour** Amber, marginally fuller.

**Nose** Sherry still, but drier. A soft whiff of alcohol.

**Body** Full.

**Palate** Sherryish. A very clean, rounded fruitness. Intense. Powerful.

**Finish** Sherry, smoke, alcohol.

### SCORE 89

## THE MACALLAN 12-year-old, 43 vol

**Colour** Amber.

**Nose** Sherry, honey, flowery notes.

**Body** Full, smooth.

**Palate** The first hints of flowering currant. Altogether more expressive.

**Finish** Slightly more rounded.

SCORE 91

## THE MACALLAN distilled 1975, bottled 1994, 43 vol

**Colour** Solid amber.

**Nose** Sherry, spices, some smokiness.

**Body** Full, rounded.

**Palate** Fresh, juicy, oaky (reminiscent of Calvados), sherry, spices, flowering currant.

**Finish** Oaky, sappy, powerful.

SCORE 94

## THE MACALLAN 25-year-old, 43 vol

**Colour** Full amber-red.

**Nose** Definite smokiness overlaying the characteristics.

**Body** Full, firm, round.

**Palate** The smokiness greatly enhances the complexity.

**Finish** Dry, complex, very long.

### SCORE 95

### Other versions of The Macallan

Independent bottlers have stayed clear of the definite article. The "As We Get It" version at cask strength and no age statement is sherryish and buttery-malty, but a little spirity. SCORE 84. A 1969 Inverallen bottling at cask strength had a bright, golden colour, a syrupy body and a very flowery, perfumy finish. SCORE 84. A 28-year-old from the same house at 55.7 vol had a fuller golden colour, a light-to-medium sherry character and a beautiful balance and complexity. SCORE 93. A 30-year-old at 52.6 vol from Cadenhead was very pale indeed, beautifully flowery, with a touch of peat. SCORE 88. Without the sherry, it is not The Macallan, but these paler bottlings show what a sweet, flowery nectar this is in any dress.

# MANNOCHMORE

**Producer** United Distillers
**Region** Highlands    **District** Speyside (Lossie)

SPEYSIDE
SINGLE MALT *SCOTCH WHISKY*

## MANNOCHMORE

*distillery* stands a few miles *south* of Elgin in *Morayshire*. The nearby *Millbuies Woods* are rich in birdlife, including the Great *Spotted* Woodpecker. The *distillery* draws process *water* from the Bardon Burn, which has its *source* in the MANNOCH HILLS, and *cooling water* from the Gedloch Burn and the *Burn of Foths*. Mannochmore *single MALT WHISKY* has a *light,fruity* aroma and a *smooth*,mellow *taste*.

AGED **12** YEARS
43% vol    Distilled & Bottled in SCOTLAND. MANNOCHMORE DISTILLERY, Elgin, Moray, Scotland.    70 cl

**T**HE MANNOCH HILLS PROVIDE water for several distilleries, including Mannochmore – one of the more modern distilleries, established in 1971–72. Its principal role has been to provide malt whisky as a component of the Haig blends, and its product has only recently become available as a single in the Flora and Fauna series. The distillery is south of Elgin, near the River Lossie. It is a close neighbour of Glenlossie. It is not unusual for distilleries to be built relatively close to one another; if the available water suits one distillery, it may also accommodate another. The same is true of other resources, the skills of local labour, and access. It is not surprising that, as in the case of Mannochmore and Glenlossie, the whiskies themselves have a family resemblance.

**House style** Fresh, flowery, dry. Aperitif.

---

**MANNOCHMORE 12-year-old, 43 vol, Flora and Fauna**

**Colour** White wine.

**Nose** Fresh. Very flowery indeed.

**Body** Medium, firm, drying on the tongue.

**Palate** Becoming lightly fruity. Clean. Dry.

**Finish** Perfumy, light, dry. Faint peat.

SCORE 72

# MILLBURN

**Producer** United Distillers
**Region** Highlands **District** Speyside (Inverness)

A S THE NIGHT TRAIN from London finishes its 11-hour journey to Inverness, the sleepy-eyed traveller glides by the distillery buildings that once housed Millburn. It was closed in 1985 and later converted into a pub and steakhouse. There are less appropriate metamorphoses, of course. The city's other two distilleries, Glen Albyn and Glen Mhor, were demolished to make room for shops.

Millburn dated at least from the beginning of licensed distilling in the Highlands, and its buildings from 1876, 1898 and 1922. The whisky has never been officially bottled, but has contributed to a vatted malt called The Mill Burn.

**House style** Smoky, aromatic. Nightcap.

### MILLBURN 1971, 40 vol, Connoisseurs Choice

| | |
|---|---|
| **Colour** Reddish-amber. | |

**Nose** Rich, aromatic, sherry start, becoming dry.

**Body** Full, smooth, quite firm.

**Palate** Sherry, malt and smokiness, in quick succession. Possibly a fraction sweeter and more aromatic than its predecessor, the 1966.

**Finish** Smoky, peaty, slowly developing into a long, warming memory of a robust malt.

SCORE 76

# MILTONDUFF

**Producer** Allied Distillers
**Region** Highlands   **District** Speyside (Lossie)

**P**LUSCARDEN PRIORY, said to have been the first site of the Miltonduff distillery, still exists. Although there is no present-day connection with the distillery, the name of the Priory is invoked on the box that houses the Miltonduff bottle. The distillery, established in 1824, was extensively modernised in the 1930s and again in the 1970s.

For a time, the company also had a Lomond still on the site. This produced a heavier malt, which was known as Mosstowie. That still has been dismantled, but the malt can be found in independent bottlings. The Miltonduff malt is well-regarded by blenders, and makes a pleasant single.

**House style** Flowery, clean, firm, elegant. Aperitif.

**MILTONDUFF 12-year-old, 43 vol**

**Colour** Soft gold.

**Nose** Fragrant, dry, flowery, with faint hints of peat and vanilla. Peatiness more evident when a little water is added.

**Body** Medium, firm, smooth.

**Palate** Sweet, very clean and delicately flowery.

**Finish** Aromatic, soothing, with some malty dryness.

SCORE 76

**MILTONDUFF 1963, 40 vol, Gordon and MacPhail**

**Colour** Amber.

**Nose** Sherryish (fino?).

**Body** Medium, smooth.

**Palate** Sherryish, sweet, some vanilla notes.

**Finish** Powerful, long. Perhaps better after dinner.

SCORE 76

**MOSSTOWIE 1975, 40 vol, Connoisseurs Choice**

**Colour** Bronze, reddish.

**Nose** Very appetising. Fresh, leafy, smoky, dry.

**Body** Medium to full, firm, oily.

**Palate** Full of flavour, with notes of leafiness, smokiness and maltiness.

**Finish** Flowery but assertive. Hints of smokiness. A hearty restorative.

SCORE 76

# MORTLACH

**Producer** United Distillers
**Region** Highlands    **District** Speyside (Dufftown)

**A**LL THE PLEASURES OF a good Speyside single malt are found in Mortlach – floweriness, peatiness, smokiness, maltiness and fruitiness – along with a good sherry character in most bottlings. The distilling water comes from springs in the Conval Hills and seems to bring a powerful taste with it. The cooling water is from the River Dullan.

There is said to have been an illicit distillery on the site; the legal one traces its history to 1823. It is very attractive, despite having been modernised in 1903 and 1964. Mortlach was the first legal distillery in Dufftown, now a very important centre for the industry. Its bottled single and those of its neighbours, Glendullan and Dufftown, arguably offer something of a local style in their robust, well-rounded attack.

**House style** Big, complex, elegant. After dinner or bedtime.

MORTLACH 16-year-old, 43 vol, Flora and Fauna

**Colour** Profound, rich, amber.

**Nose** Dry oloroso sherry. Smoky, peaty.

**Body** Medium to full, firm, smooth.

**Palate** Sherryish, smoky, peaty, sappy, some fruitiness, assertive.

**Finish** Long and dry.

SCORE 81

## MORTLACH 15-year-old, 40 vol

**Colour** Medium amber.

**Nose** Smoky, malty, fresh sherry. Very aromatic.

**Body** Medium to full, rich.

**Palate** Smokiness. Heathery, resiny notes, succulent maltiness, fruitiness (juicy pears), sherry, oak.

**Finish** Perfumy, long, dry.

SCORE 81

## MORTLACH 21-year-old, 40 vol, Gordon and MacPhail

**Colour** Amber.

**Nose** Sherry. Dry oloroso? Clean, powerful, rich, delicious.

**Body** Medium to full, rounded.

**Palate** Sherryish at first, then very smoky. As arousing to the senses as a log fire.

**Finish** Long, round, dry.

SCORE 81

# NORTH PORT

**Producer** United Distillers
**Region** Highlands **District** Eastern Highlands

CONNOISSEURS CHOICE

*Connoisseurs Choice, a range of single malts from various districts of Scotland*

*In the Highlands are situated the greatest number of malt whisky distilleries.*

SINGLE HIGHLAND
MALT SCOTCH WHISKY
DISTILLED AT
NORTH PORT-BRECHIN
DISTILLERY
*Proprietors: Mitchel Bros. Ltd*

DISTILLED **1974** DISTILLED

SPECIALLY SELECTED, PRODUCED AND BOTTLED BY
70cl **GORDON & MACPHAIL** 40%vol
ELGIN · SCOTLAND
PRODUCT OF SCOTLAND

T HE NAME INDICATES THE NORTH GATE of the small, once-walled city of Brechin. The distillery was built in 1820. The pioneering whisky writer, Alfred Barnard, who toured Scotland's distilleries in the 1880s, recorded that this one obtained its barley from the farmers around Brechin, and its peat and water from the Grampian mountains. The present-day whisky historian, Derek Cooper, reports that the condensers were cooled in a stream that ran through the distillery. North Port was modernised in the 1970s and closed in 1983. It has now been sold for re-development. Its whisky can still be found in independent bottlings.

**House style** Dry, astringent. Aperitif.

### NORTH PORT 1974, 40 vol, Connoisseurs Choice

**Colour** Full gold to amber.

**Nose** Fragrant, dry, lightly smoky.

**Body** Light to medium. Light oiliness. Smooth.

**Palate** Sweetish. Sherryish. Light oiliness. Saltiness, smokiness. Becoming dry, with some astringency, and falling away somewhat.

**Finish** Dry, sharp and warming.

SCORE 66

# OBAN

**Producer** United Distillers
**Region** Highlands   **District** Western Highlands

I F THE WESTERN HIGHLANDS has a capital, it is the town of Oban. If the region has a classic malt, it is the one bearing the town's name. The western Highlands mainland does not have many distilleries, but its whiskies tend to be well-rounded and malty, with some smokiness.

This is still a thinly populated part of Scotland. The first settlers arrived by sea and came to this coast in 5000 BC, making their homes in caves in the cliffside. That story, and a later account of Scottish invasion from Antrim in Ireland, are told on the label of the 14-year-old Oban, in "The Classic Malts" series offered by United Distillers. This version is replacing the 12-year-old, which was put into a bottle that looked as though it contained perfume.

The traveller returning from the islands of Mull or Iona, or from Fingal's Cave, sees Oban as a Victorian town, with the distillery growing out of those cliffside caves. The distillery is said to have been founded in 1794, though the present buildings probably date from the 1880s. The stillhouse was rebuilt in the late 1960s and early 1970s, and there was further work in 1991. The Oban malt whisky has contributed to the various John Hopkins blends, including one that is romantically called "Old Mull".

**House style** Medium, with fresh peat and a whiff of the sea. With seafood or game, or after dinner.

*"The gateway to the Isles", the ferry town of Oban has a distillery producing a malt with a definite coast and island character.*

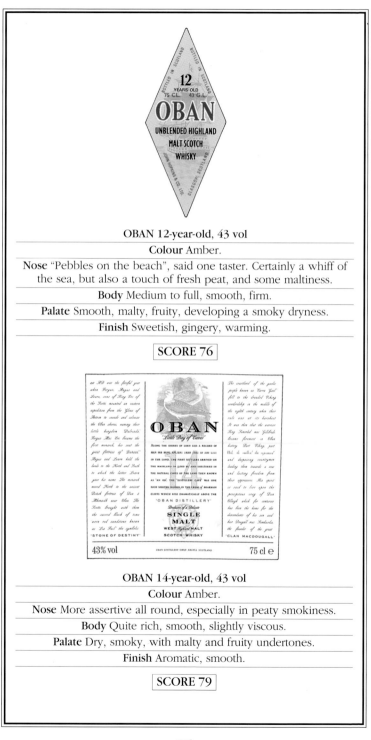

OBAN 12-year-old, 43 vol

Colour Amber.

Nose "Pebbles on the beach", said one taster. Certainly a whiff of the sea, but also a touch of fresh peat, and some maltiness.

Body Medium to full, smooth, firm.

Palate Smooth, malty, fruity, developing a smoky dryness.

Finish Sweetish, gingery, warming.

SCORE 76

OBAN 14-year-old, 43 vol

Colour Amber.

Nose More assertive all round, especially in peaty smokiness.

Body Quite rich, smooth, slightly viscous.

Palate Dry, smoky, with malty and fruity undertones.

Finish Aromatic, smooth.

SCORE 79

# PITTYVAICH

**Producer** United Distillers
**Region** Highlands   **District** Speyside (Dufftown)

SPEYSIDE
SINGLE MALT
*SCOTCH WHISKY*

**PITTYVAICH**

*distillery* is situated in the
*DULLAN GLEN* on the outskirts
of Dufftown, near to the *historic*
*Mortlach Church* which dates back
to the ⑨ᵗʰ. The distillery draws
water from two nearby

springs - *CONVALLEYS* and
*BALLIEMORE*. Pittyvaich single
MALT SCOTCH WHISKY
has a *perfumed, fruity*
nose and a robust flavour with
a hint of *spiciness.*

A G E D **12** Y E A R S

43% vol 70 cl

**O**NE OF THE NEWEST DISTILLERIES, built by Bell's in 1975. In the late 1980s, enthusiasts for single malts began to wonder whether the product would become available to them. Then independent bottler James MacArthur released a 12-year-old revealing a perfumy, soft-pear house character. The same bottler has since added a 14-year-old that more assertively pronounces its dry finish. A bottling of the same age from the Scotch Malt Whisky Society was similar but seemed to have more spicy dryness on the nose. None of these bore obvious signs of sherry ageing. In 1991 there was finally an official bottling, at 12 years old, in United's Flora and Fauna series. This has all the other characteristics, plus a hefty dose of sherry. There have since been several independent bottlings. The distillery is currently mothballed.

**House style** Fruity, oily, spicy, spirity. After dinner – a Scottish grappa, so to speak.

| PITTYVAICH 12-year-old, 43 vol, Flora and Fauna |
|---|
| **Colour** Deep amber-red. |
| **Nose** Sherryish, perfumy, pear-skin. |
| **Body** Medium. |
| **Palate** Very sherryish. Assertive. Some malty chewiness. Soft, sweet, pear-like fruitiness, moving to a spicy dryness. |
| **Finish** Spicy, perfumy, intensely dry, lingering. |
| SCORE 69 |

# PORT ELLEN

**Producer** United Distillers
**Region** Islay   **District** South shore

T HE RAREST OF ISLAY MALTS. The distillery, founded in the 1820s and expanded in the 1960s, was closed temporarily in the 1980s. Its closure now seems permanent. The distillery's white-painted warehouses form an attractive street close to the sea in Port Ellen, one of the three principal villages on Islay.

Adjoining the distillery is a modern maltings, issuing pungent peat smoke lest anyone requires reminding of the island's preoccupation. The malt goes to two other Islay distilleries owned by United Distillers, Lagavulin and Caol Ila.

**House style** Seaweedy, peppery, salty. Nightcap.

**PORT ELLEN 12-year-old, 63.8 vol, Cadenhead**

| **Colour** White wine. |
| --- |
| **Nose** Powerful, appetising and arousing to the senses. Earthy, hugely seaweedy, sour and peppery. |
| **Body** Medium, firm. |
| **Palate** Surging with flavours. Salty, seaweedy, sweet-and-sour, and an explosion of pepper. |
| **Finish** Peppery, salty, almost sandy. |

SCORE 79

## PORT ELLEN 13-year-old, 43 vol, Master of Malt

**Colour** Pale gold.

**Nose** Drier, more oily and more tightly combined aromas.

**Body** Medium, smooth.

**Palate** Peppery, very spicy, oily.

**Finish** Very dry. Sea notes. Wood notes.

### SCORE 79

## PORT ELLEN 1977, 40 vol, Connoisseurs Choice

**Colour** Oily, amber.

**Nose** Astonishing sea air, brineyness, pepper, spices, vanilla, perfuminess. Oily notes.

**Body** Medium, soft.

**Palate** Soft, becoming spicy, with pepper.

**Finish** Very spicy, peppery, explosive.

### SCORE 80

## PORT ELLEN 1974, 56.4 vol, Signatory

**Colour** Very pale gold.

**Nose** Oily.

**Body** Medium, soft.

**Palate** Dry, smooth, peppery.

**Finish** Very dry. Remarkably warming. Very long.

### SCORE 80

# OLD PULTENEY

**Producer** Allied Distillers
**Region** Highlands   **District** Northern Highlands

NOWN AS "THE MANZANILLA OF THE NORTH" for its salty tang. The producers of Manzanilla do supply casks to the Scotch whisky industry, and it is certainly possible that the odd butt has accommodated a charge of Pulteney whisky, but in general the owners are more inclined towards Bourbon wood. The saltiness probably owes more to the sea-air. Not only is the Pulteney distillery on the coast, its site is so exposed as to be falling off the furthest end of Scotland.

Pulteney was founded in 1826 and rebuilt by the Hiram Walker company in 1959 as a contributor of malt whisky to the Ballantine blends.

**House style** Fresh, salty, appetising. Pre-dinner.

---

**OLD PULTENEY 8-year-old, 40 vol, Gordon and MacPhail**

| |
|---|
| **Colour** Amber. |
| **Nose** Fresh, dry, with a hint of sea air. |
| **Body** Light, firm. |
| **Palate** Faintly salty, earthy-spicy, appetising, smooth, becoming gently malty. |
| **Finish** Salty, tangy, warming, soothing, long. |

**SCORE 77**

**Other versions of Old Pulteney**
A 15-year-old at 40 vol from Gordon and MacPhail had a lovely balance of sherry and saltiness. SCORE 79. A 17-year-old at 52.8 vol, labelled Whalligoe, was lightly smooth and very salty. SCORE 78. A 1961 at 40 vol from Gordon and MacPhail was more sherryish, but still well-balanced. SCORE 79.

# ROSEBANK

**Producer** United Distillers
**Region** Lowland   **District** Central Lowlands

T**HE CLASSIC LOWLAND MALT** in the view of some devotees, though others favour Auchentoshan, Bladnoch, Glenkinchie or Littlemill. There was an outcry when Bladnoch and Rosebank were mothballed in 1993, and much scepticism as to whether they would reopen.

Like Auchentoshan, Rosebank has been cherished for its Lowland tradition of triple-distillation. The distillery is at Cemelon, Falkirk, on the Forth–Clyde canal. Its origins may be as early as 1817 and some buildings from the 1850s and 1860s survive, straddling the main road.

Although a light Lowlander might be expected to perform best with youth on its side, the pot-pourri aroma and flowery palate have survived splendidly in a recent rush of more mature releases from independent bottlers, even a 25-year-old malt from Signatory.

**House style** Aromatic, with suggestions of clover. Aperitif.

| ROSEBANK 8-year-old, 40 vol |
|---|
| **Colour** Amber. |
| **Nose** Dry, grassy-flowery, pot-pourri aroma. Hint of dryish sherry. |
| **Body** Light, but very smooth. |
| **Palate** Dry, flowery, fruity. Becomes much less dry when water is added. |
| **Finish** Dry. |

SCORE 76

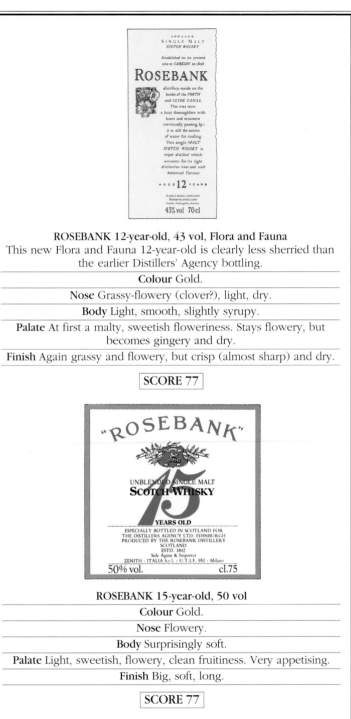

**ROSEBANK 12-year-old, 43 vol, Flora and Fauna**
This new Flora and Fauna 12-year-old is clearly less sherried than the earlier Distillers' Agency bottling.

**Colour** Gold.

**Nose** Grassy-flowery (clover?), light, dry.

**Body** Light, smooth, slightly syrupy.

**Palate** At first a malty, sweetish floweriness. Stays flowery, but becomes gingery and dry.

**Finish** Again grassy and flowery, but crisp (almost sharp) and dry.

SCORE 77

**ROSEBANK 15-year-old, 50 vol**

**Colour** Gold.

**Nose** Flowery.

**Body** Surprisingly soft.

**Palate** Light, sweetish, flowery, clean fruitiness. Very appetising.

**Finish** Big, soft, long.

SCORE 77

# ST MAGDALENE

**Producer** United Distillers
**Region** Lowland    **District** Central Lowlands

HIS SITE ACCOMMODATED a leper colony in the twelfth century, and later a convent, before a distillery was established, possibly in the late 1700s. Production ceased in about 1983 and some of the buildings have since been converted into apartments. The distillery has sometimes been known as Linlithgow, after its home town, west of Edinburgh and close to the River Forth.

**House style** Perfumy, grassy, smooth. Restorative.

### ST MAGDALENE 1965, 40 vol, Connoisseurs Choice

| | |
|---|---|
| **Colour** | Amber-red. |
| **Nose** | Sherry. Very perfumy. Grassy, faintly smoky. Slightly oaky. |
| **Body** | Light to medium. Soft. Smooth. |
| **Palate** | More perfumy than the 1964. Less of the "grassy bonfire", but it is still there. |
| **Finish** | Dry but soft. Warming, gentle. |

### SCORE 68

**Other versions of St Magdalene**

A 10-year-old (1982) from Cadenhead at 61.6 vol was the colour of white wine, grassy, with both sweetness and phenol on the nose, and much the same in the palate, over an oily body. SCORE 68. Another cask at the same age, again from Cadenhead, emerged at 62.3 vol. It was similar, but more restrained, flowery, and sweeter. SCORE 68.

# SCAPA

**Producer** Allied Distillers
**Region** Highlands   **Island** Orkney

S CAPA FLOW, A STRETCH OF WATER linking the North Sea to the Atlantic, is famous for its roles in both World Wars. The distillery, near Kirkwall, fails to be the northernmost in Scotland by only half a mile. It was founded in 1885, and was powered by a waterwheel that has now been restored. Two of the original warehouses survive, accommodating empty casks, but most of the present fabric dates from 1959.

The water supply is very peaty, but the distillery uses wholly unpeated malt. It has a Lomond wash-still, which may contribute to a slight oiliness of the whisky. Maturation is in Bourbon casks, and that may account for the vanilla notes, sometimes suggesting very spicy chocolate – or licorice of the salty style made in the Netherlands.

**House style** Salt, hay. Oily, spicy chocolate. Aperitif.

**SCAPA 8-year-old, 40 vol, Gordon and MacPhail**
After a hearty walk, before dinner.

| Colour Amber. |
| --- |
| **Nose** Fresh, sea-breeze saltiness, new-mown hay, heather, some Bourbon character. |
| **Body** Medium, silky. |
| **Palate** Salty, slightly sharp, tangy. |
| **Finish** Oily but dry, appetising. |

SCORE 76

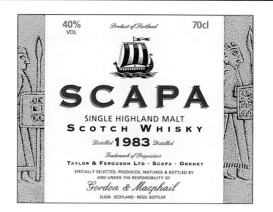

### SCAPA 1983, 40 vol, Gordon and MacPhail

**Colour** Amber.

**Nose** Salt, hay, chocolate, Bourbon.

**Body** Medium, silky.

**Palate** Smooth, vanilla, chocolate. Tangy towards finish.

**Finish** Chocolate, toffee, licorice, salt.

### SCORE 78

### SCAPA 24-year-old, 46.5 vol, Cadenhead
(Distilled 1965, bottled 1990)

**Colour** Gold.

**Nose** Salty and sharp. Appetising.

**Body** Medium, soft, smooth.

**Palate** Salty, hay-like, heathery, perfumy.

**Finish** Salty, appetite-arousing.

### SCORE 77

### SCAPA 1963, 40 vol, Gordon and MacPhail
A nightcap.

**Colour** Full amber.

**Nose** Powerful. Wonderfully briny.

**Body** Medium, soft, smooth.

**Palate** Salty and sharp, but also with caramelly Bourbon and bitter-chocolate notes.

**Finish** Bitter-chocolate, long, sustaining.

### SCORE 79

# THE SINGLETON

**Producer** IDV/Justerini and Brooks
**Region** Highlands    **District** Speyside

"A DESIGNER WHISKY" said the cynics when The Singleton was launched as a bottled malt in 1986. The brand name, seeking to imply a certain singularity, was (and is) contrived, ostensibly because the producers felt that the name of the distillery, Auchroisk (pronounced "othroysk") was too difficult for the prospective consumer. In Gaelic it means "ford across the red stream", and lies on the Mulben burn, which flows into the Spey. A spring, producing very soft water' was the reason the site was chosen. The whisky is sweet, with a hint of aniseed, as evidenced by some Cadenhead bottlings from plain wood under the Auchroisk name. Vintages such as The Singleton are released at more than 10 years, and at 12-plus, with a substantial degree of sherry ageing.

**House style** Softly spicy. Liqueurish. After dinner.

### THE SINGLETON 1981, 40 vol

| | |
|---|---|
| **Colour** Amber. |
| **Nose** Sherry, malt, licorice, aniseed, a hint of peat. |
| **Body** Medium. Very smooth. |
| **Palate** Licorice, aniseed, toffee, sherry. |
| **Finish** Liqueurish, with a lightly smoky background. |

### SCORE 79

# SPEYBURN

**Producer** Inver House
**Region** Highlands    **District** Speyside (Rothes)

T HERE ARE MANY CLAIMANTS to being the most beautifully situated distillery in Scotland, and Speyburn is surely one of them. This handsome Victorian distillery, set in a deep sweeping valley, makes a spectacular sight on the road between Rothes and Elgin. It was built in 1897 and, despite modernisations, has not undergone dramatic change.

In the early 1990s, Speyburn was acquired by Inver House, whose 10-year-old is replacing the similar 12-year-old released in the Flora and Fauna series by the previous owners.

**House style** Flowery, herbal, heathery. Aperitif.

*Set in a hollow in the rolling hills of the Spey valley, the Speyburn distillery produces an all-too-rare characterful malt.*

## SPEYBURN 10-year-old, 40 vol

**Colour** Solid gold.

**Nose** Flowery.

**Body** Medium, gentle.

**Palate** Clean, lightly malty. Developing fresh, herbal, heathery notes.

**Finish** Fresh, very sweet, lightly syrupy.

### SCORE 71

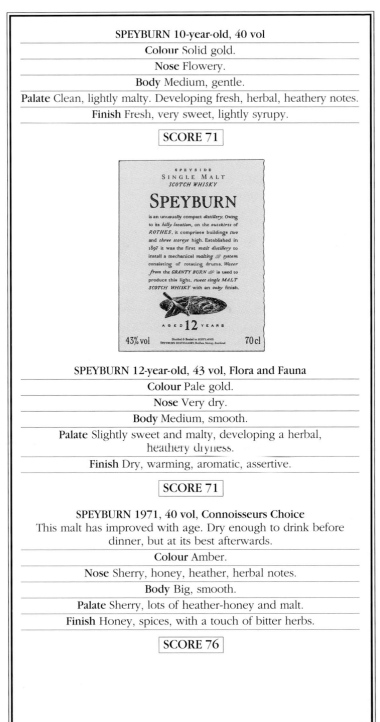

SPEYSIDE
SINGLE MALT
*SCOTCH WHISKY*

# SPEYBURN

is an unusually compact *distillery*. Owing to its *hilly location*, on the *outskirts of ROTHES*, it comprises buildings *two* and *three storeys* high. Established in 1897 it was the first *malt distillery* to install a mechanical *malting system* consisting of rotating drums. *Water from the GRANTY BURN* is used to produce this light, *sweet single MALT SCOTCH WHISKY* with an *oaky* finish.

AGED **12** YEARS

43% vol     Distilled & Bottled in SCOTLAND.
SPEYBURN DISTILLERY, Rothes, Moray, Scotland.     70cl

## SPEYBURN 12-year-old, 43 vol, Flora and Fauna

**Colour** Pale gold.

**Nose** Very dry.

**Body** Medium, smooth.

**Palate** Slightly sweet and malty, developing a herbal, heathery dryness.

**Finish** Dry, warming, aromatic, assertive.

### SCORE 71

## SPEYBURN 1971, 40 vol, Connoisseurs Choice

This malt has improved with age. Dry enough to drink before dinner, but at its best afterwards.

**Colour** Amber.

**Nose** Sherry, honey, heather, herbal notes.

**Body** Big, smooth.

**Palate** Sherry, lots of heather-honey and malt.

**Finish** Honey, spices, with a touch of bitter herbs.

### SCORE 76

# SPRINGBANK

**Producer** J. and A. Mitchell
**Region** Campbeltown

THE CLASSIC CAMPBELTOWN malts are those produced and matured by the Springbank distillery, and they have, over the years, appeared in a wide variety of ages. The single malt, Longrow, has been made at the same distillery, but less frequently, and in fewer ages. It may be produced more often in the future.

Springbank is made from a barley-malt of medium peatiness, using an unusual configuration of the distillery's three stills. Effectively, it is distilled two and a half times, which makes for a more refined whisky. Longrow is made from a malt that is wholly peat-dried, but the spirit is distilled by the more conventional double method.

Although Campbeltown has had 30 distilleries, most closed by the 1930s. Several stood together on a street called Longrow. One was also called Longrow, from 1824 to 1896, and one of its warehouses survives as the bottling hall at Springbank. This gives a bittersweet validity to the notion of Springbank producing a second whisky called Longrow.

Campbeltown grows a small amount of barley, and Springbank once used this in its own maltings; a new generation of management would like to do so again. The town's maltsters once cut local peat, and Springbank has an ambition to find new supplies in the area. Local coal once fuelled Springbank's stills, but the mine closed in the late 1960s. The last Springbank malt to employ all three local materials was released under the subtitle West Highland, 25 years later, and it can still sometimes be sighted.

Springbank's floor-maltings have made a major contribution to its whiskies, especially the peaty Longrow. The maltings closed in the late 1970s, but were restored to production in 1992. The Longrow being made now will be ready to drink around 2010. At that point, it may be Scotland's finest whisky.

Glenfiddich and Springbank are the only distilleries to bottle their whiskies on site. Springbank has been able to do this because the company also owns the independent bottler Cadenhead, giving Springbank access to a wide variety of casks. These have even included rum casks, which imparted a distinctively mint-toffee note to the whisky.

**Springbank house style** Salty, oily, coconut. Aperitif.

**Longrow house style** Piney, oily, damp earth. Nightcap.

## SPRINGBANK 12-year-old, 46 vol

**Colour** White wine.

**Nose** Salty, grassy, leafy.

**Body** Light to medium, smooth.

**Palate** Very salty, lightly oily, with very long development to fruity and sweet notes.

**Finish** Both briny and sweet. Very appetising.

SCORE 84

## SPRINGBANK 15-year-old, 46 vol

**Colour** Solid amber.

**Nose** Brine, slight peat, tar, sherry.

**Body** Medium to full. Very oily.

**Palate** Salt, coconut, toffee.

**Finish** Very lively and satisfying.

SCORE 88

**SPRINGBANK 21-year-old, 46 vol**

**Colour** Full amber.

**Nose** Sherry, brine, some wood.

**Body** Medium to full. Firm.

**Palate** Restrained salt, more coconut, nut-toffee.

**Finish** Salty, some peat, sappy, oaky.

SCORE 87

A 1972, of perhaps the same age, was less sherried and therefore less woody, more complex and gentler.

**SPRINGBANK 25-year-old, 46 vol**

**Colour** Amber.

**Nose** Salty, whiff of peat, some wood.

**Body** Medium, smooth.

**Palate** Intensely aromatic coconut notes, moving to walnut and sherry. Some tasters have found bananas, others seed cake.

**Finish** Powerful, sherry, oak, salt. Long, lingering.

SCORE 88

### SPRINGBANK 30-year-old, 46 vol

**Colour** Very deep amber-red, with orangey highlights. Very attractive.

**Nose** Sherry, raisins, oak.

**Body** Full, syrupy.

**Palate** Sherry, raisins, butterscotch, butter itself, salt. Very concentrated flavours.

**Finish** Oaky, sappy, peaty, salty.

SCORE 92

### SPRINGBANK West Highland, 1966, 58.1 vol

**Colour** Brownish-red, almost mahogany.

**Nose** Oaky. Heavily sherried. Smoky, but still fragrant, with a hint of (salty?) sharpness.

**Body** Big, tongue-coating.

**Palate** Sherry at first, then oak, with sappiness and saltiness emerging somewhere; coconut and then a cough-syrup soothing quality.

**Finish** More sherry, balanced by an oaky dryness, then cough-syrup again. Very long, soothing and digestif.

SCORE 93

### LONGROW 1974, 46 vol

**Colour** Full gold.

**Nose** Pungent, piney, earthy, peaty.

**Body** Medium, oily.

**Palate** Sweet coconut, oiliness, distinctively piney, phenolic, peaty.

**Finish** Salty, intense, tenacious, distinctive, long.

SCORE 90

# STRATHISLA

**Producer** Seagram/Chivas Brothers
**Region** Highland **District** Speyside (Strathisla)

T HE OLDEST DISTILLERY in the north of Scotland. In the 13th century, Dominican monks used a spring nearby to provide water for brewing beer. The same water, with a touch of calcium hardness and scarcely any peat character, has been used in the distillation of whisky since at least 1786. Strathisla, which has also at times been known as Milltown, began its life as a farm distillery. It started to take its present shape from the 1820s onwards, especially after a fire in 1876. In 1950 it was acquired by Seagram.

Lightly peated malt is used, as well as wooden wash-backs and small stills, two of them coal-fired. Although wooden wash-backs are by no means unusual, Strathisla believes that fermentation characteristics play a very important part in the character of its dry, fruity, oaky, malt whisky. The only official bottling is the 12-year-old, but a range of ages is bottled under the distillery's name by Gordon and MacPhail.

**House style** Dry, fruity. After dinner.

**STRATHISLA 8-year-old, 40 vol, Gordon and MacPhail**

| |
|---|
| **Colour** Amber. |
| **Nose** Dry, sherryish. Quite complex. |
| **Body** Medium, firm. |
| **Palate** Dry maltiness, developing to sweeter notes, with cereal-grain and sherry character. |
| **Finish** Big, dry, slightly sappy, lingering. |

SCORE 79

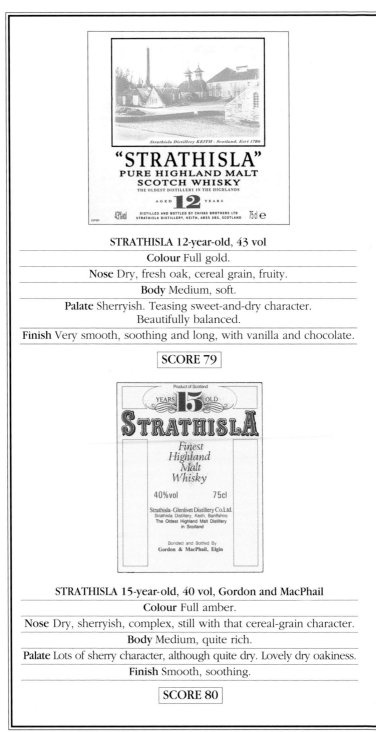

**STRATHISLA 12-year-old, 43 vol**

| |
|---|
| **Colour** Full gold. |
| **Nose** Dry, fresh oak, cereal grain, fruity. |
| **Body** Medium, soft. |
| **Palate** Sherryish. Teasing sweet-and-dry character. Beautifully balanced. |
| **Finish** Very smooth, soothing and long, with vanilla and chocolate. |

SCORE 79

**STRATHISLA 15-year-old, 40 vol, Gordon and MacPhail**

| |
|---|
| **Colour** Full amber. |
| **Nose** Dry, sherryish, complex, still with that cereal-grain character. |
| **Body** Medium, quite rich. |
| **Palate** Lots of sherry character, although quite dry. Lovely dry oakiness. |
| **Finish** Smooth, soothing. |

SCORE 80

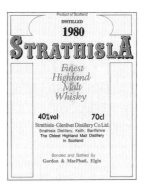

**STRATHISLA 1980, 40 vol, Gordon and MacPhail**

**Colour** Amber.

**Nose** Complex, with lots of soft, fruity notes; honey, sherry, oak and a touch of peat.

**Body** Medium but rich.

**Palate** Distinctive and delicious. Beginning with sherry and honey, and moving towards fruity dryness.

**Finish** Dry but soothing.

SCORE 80

**STRATHISLA 20-year-old, 46 vol, Cadenhead**

**Colour** Rich amber-red. Very dark indeed.

**Nose** Powerful, sweet, juicy, sherry aroma, but still the oak and the whisky make themselves known underneath all of this.

**Body** Very rich.

**Palate** Rich, raisiny, sherry character at first, followed by the oakiness and the spirit itself.

**Finish** Lots of sherry, and very warming. Earns points for daring to be so heavily sherried.

SCORE 76

STRATHISLA 1967, 40 vol, Gordon and MacPhail

**Colour** Full amber.

**Nose** Fresh oak, sap, sherry, gentler fruit, peat.

**Body** Medium, smooth, firm.

**Palate** Depth of fruity, spicy flavours. Sherry. Oak. Flavours tightly combined.

**Finish** Big, fresh oak, peat, hint of heather. A beautifully complex whisky, just the right side of woodiness.

SCORE 81

STRATHISLA 1960, 40 vol, Gordon and MacPhail

**Colour** Amber-red.

**Nose** Oaky, still fruity, with a touch of peat.

**Body** Medium to full. Firm.

**Palate** Buttery, vanilla-like, sherry. Good fruitiness, some peat.

**Finish** Oaky, sappy, slightly bitter. Dry.

SCORE 78

**STRATHISLA 35-year-old, 40 vol, Gordon and MacPhail**

**Colour** Full gold.

**Nose** Some welcome smokiness.

**Body** Soft, smooth.

**Palate** Light, sweetish.

**Finish** Light, smooth. Less sherryish than its closest peers, but mellow.

SCORE 75

**STRATHISLA 1958, 40 vol, Gordon and MacPhail**

**Colour** Amber-brown.

**Nose** Woody.

**Body** Medium to full, smooth.

**Palate** Oaky and dry, but still some butteriness coming through.

**Finish** Oaky, drying on the tongue.

SCORE 76

# STRATHMILL

**Producer** IDV/Justerini and Brooks
**Region** Highlands   **District** Speyside (Strathisla)

 HE TOWN OF KEITH must once have been a considerable grain-milling centre. The Glen Keith distillery was built on the site of a corn mill. Strathmill, as its name suggests, went one better. It was rebuilt from a corn mill, in 1891, when the whisky industry was having one of its periodic upswings. Three years later, it was acquired by W. and A. Gilbey, which became a part of International Distillers and Vintners, which, in turn, was taken over by Watney's. Watney's was later bought by Grandmet, of which Justerini and Brooks is a subsidiary. Arguably, the distillery has been in the same ownership for a century, but its whisky does not seem to have been available as a single until a bottling of the 1980 by the wine merchant chain Oddbins in 1993. This lusciously sweet version was quickly followed by a similar bottling of the same year from Cadenhead.

**House style** The whisky world's answer to orange muscat.

| STRATHMILL 11-year-old, 60.6 vol, Cadenhead |
| --- |
| **Colour** Pale gold, with a greenish cast. Oily, refractive. |
| **Nose** Sweet, suggestions of orange rind. |
| **Body** Medium to full, syrupy. |
| **Palate** Soft, syrupy, orange rind, fruity, honeyish. |
| **Finish** Syrupy, creamy, developing to surge of orange zest. |

SCORE 77

# TALISKER

**Producer** United Distillers
**Region** Highlands    **Island** Skye

O NE OF THE MOST INDIVIDUALISTIC of single malts, with a powerful palate and an emphatic island character. What the bigger examples of Zinfandel are to wine, Talisker is to single malts. It has a distinctively peppery character, so hot as to make one taster's temples steam. The phrase "explodes on the palate" is among the descriptions used by blenders at United Distillers; surely they had Talisker in mind when they composed this. "The lava of the Cuillins" was another taster's response. The Cuillins are the dramatic hills of Skye, the island home of Talisker. The distillery is on the west coast of the island, on the shores of Loch Harport.

After a number of false starts on other sites, the distillery was established in 1831 and expanded in 1900. For much of its life, it used triple-distillation, and in those days Robert Louis Stevenson ranked Talisker as a style on its own, comparable with the Islay and Glenlivet whiskies. It switched to double-distillation in 1928, and was partly rebuilt in 1960.

Its 8-year-old bottled single malt has been replaced by a 10-year-old, which is featured in the United Distillers' "Classic Malts" range. Some malt-lovers prefer the dry assertiveness of Talisker at the lesser age, although the older version does have a fuller, more rounded character. A 14-year-old at 64.4 vol from Cadenhead, apparently without sherry, was full of sea-air, seaweed and pepper on the nose, and explosively peppery and salty in palate. A 15-year-old, from the same bottler at 56.4 vol was yellowy-brown, heavily sherried and dominated at first by the cask, but then followed by an astonishingly long development of distillery flavours. A 1955 at 53.6 vol from Gordon and MacPhail had a brighter, but still deep, amber-red colour. It seemed to have slightly less sherry and more oak, but again had considerable development.

Although Talisker is the only distillery on Skye, the island is also home to a company making a vatted malt called Poit Dubh, and a blend, Te Bheag. Both are said to contain some Talisker, and their hearty palates seem to support this suggestion. A dry, perfumy, blended whisky called Isle of Skye is made by the Edinburgh merchants Ian Macleod and Co. The style of whisky liqueur represented by Drambuie is also said to have originated on Skye.

**House style** Volcanic. A winter warmer.

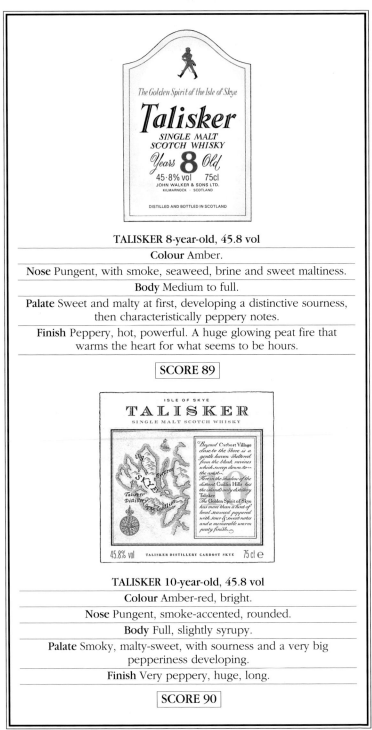

**TALISKER 8-year-old, 45.8 vol**

**Colour** Amber.

**Nose** Pungent, with smoke, seaweed, brine and sweet maltiness.

**Body** Medium to full.

**Palate** Sweet and malty at first, developing a distinctive sourness, then characteristically peppery notes.

**Finish** Peppery, hot, powerful. A huge glowing peat fire that warms the heart for what seems to be hours.

SCORE 89

**TALISKER 10-year-old, 45.8 vol**

**Colour** Amber-red, bright.

**Nose** Pungent, smoke-accented, rounded.

**Body** Full, slightly syrupy.

**Palate** Smoky, malty-sweet, with sourness and a very big pepperiness developing.

**Finish** Very peppery, huge, long.

SCORE 90

# TAMDHU

**Producer** Highland Distilleries
**Region** Highlands  **District** Speyside

T HE PRINCIPAL SPEYSIDE PRODUCT among the bottled single malts in the Highland Distilleries range. A mild, urbane whisky, leaning towards malty sweetness.

The distillery is in the heart of Speyside, between Knockando and Cardhu. It was founded in 1896 and largely rebuilt in the 1970s. Water comes from the Tamdhu burn, which flows through woodland into the Spey. Tamdhu has a sizable and impressive Saladin maltings. The distillery is impeccably well kept, and has its own touches of tradition, notably its enthusiasm for wooden fermenting vessels.

The whisky is becoming better known as a bottled single malt and is a component of The Famous Grouse blend. At barrel proof, it has performed especially well in Scotch Malt Whisky Society bottlings.

**House style** Mild, urbane, toffee-nosed. Versatile, but best after dinner.

**Tamdhu** GLENLIVET
*Scotch*
**Malt Whisky**
40% vol                    75 cl
100% SCOTCH WHISKY · PRODUCT OF SCOTLAND
*Distilled by*
THE HIGHLAND DISTILLERIES CO. LTD.
TAMDHU — GLENLIVET DISTILLERY
KNOCKANDO · MORAYSHIRE
*Bottled by*
GORDON & MACPHAIL · ELGIN · SCOTLAND
REGD. BOTTLER

| TAMDHU 8-year-old, 40 vol, Gordon and MacPhail |
|---|
| **Colour** Amber. |
| **Nose** Light, sweetish, malty. Some sherry character. |
| **Body** Light to medium. |
| **Palate** Sweetish, slightly toffeeish malt character, developing towards some peaty dryness. |
| **Finish** Smoky, then returning to malty sweetness. |

SCORE 75

## TAMDHU 10-year-old, 40 vol

**Colour** Pale amber.

**Nose** Perhaps a dash smokier.

**Body** Light to medium, rounded.

**Palate** Fragrant perfuminess. Toffeeish and malty, without being rich.

**Finish** Mellow, complete.

### SCORE 75

## TAMDHU 15-year-old, 43 vol

**Colour** Amber.

**Nose** Full, appetising. Definite sherry character.

**Body** Light to medium, firm.

**Palate** Accent on malty sweetness, but with a nice balance of aromatic, cedary smokiness. Lots of character, but this becomes evident only after a period of acquaintance. This is a restrained, well-balanced malt.

**Finish** Beautifully rounded. A gentle after-dinner whisky.

### SCORE 76

## TAMDHU, no age statement, 40 vol

**Colour** Full gold.

**Nose** Malty, toffeeish, hint of peat.

**Body** Light to medium, rounded.

**Palate** Toffeeish, with developing sweetness.

**Finish** Malty, sweet, satisfying.

### SCORE 74

# TAMNAVULIN

**Producer** Invergordon
**Region** Highlands   **District** Speyside (Livet)

R IGHT ON THE LITTLE RIVER LIVET, on the steep side of the glen. Among the malts that are produced in the parish of Glenlivet, this is the lightest in body, although not in palate. In taste, it is a little more assertive than Tomintoul, with which it might be most closely compared.

The distillery's location favours a different spelling, Tomnavoulin, but such discrepancies are hardly unusual in Scotland. The name means "mill on the hill", and part of the premises was formerly used for the carding of wool. The distillery, built in the 1960s, has a somewhat utilitarian look, but makes an elegant malt that is a delightful aperitif. Look out for occasional bottlings of especially good vintages under the rubric "Stillman's Dram".

**House style** Aromatic, herbal. Aperitif.

| TAMNAVULIN 10-year-old, 43 vol |
|---|
| **Colour** White wine. |
| **Nose** Very aromatic. A touch of peat, hay, heather, herbal notes. Slightly medicinal. |
| **Body** Light but smooth. |
| **Palate** Lemon, flowering currant. Winey. |
| **Finish** Aromatic. Juniper? |
| SCORE 76 |

PRODUCT OF SCOTLAND
**SINGLE MALT SCOTCH WHISKY**
from
# Tamnavulin-Glenlivet
**Distillery**
Proprietors:
Tamnavulin-Glenlivet Distillery Co. Ltd.

Bottled by Wm. Cadenhead,
75 cl     18 Golden Square, Aberdeen     46% vol
Scotland

## TAMNAVULIN 20-year-old, 46 vol, Cadenhead

**Colour** Deep amber.

**Nose** Powerful sherry, with some dryness behind.

**Body** Light to medium.

**Palate** Sherryish, gingery, lemony, sappy.

**Finish** Overwhelmingly sappy and oaky, even after considerable dilution.

### SCORE 64

# TEANINICH

**Producer** United Distillers
**Region** Highlands   **District** Northern Highlands

A WELL-MADE ASSERTIVE malt in the earthy style of the Northern Highlands. The distillery, near Alness was founded in 1817 and extended in 1899. In 1970, a new stillhouse was constructed. With its six stills visible from the road, it looks very modern. It closed in the mid-1980s, but reopened in 1991. A Flora and Fauna version is a welcome addition to the various independent bottlings.

**House style** Robust, toffeeish, spicy, leafy. Restorative or after dinner.

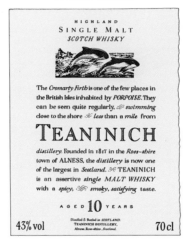

HIGHLAND
SINGLE MALT
*SCOTCH WHISKY*

The *Cromarty Firth* is one of the few places in the British Isles inhabited by *PORPOISE*. They can be seen quite regularly, *& swimming* close to the shore *& less* than a *mile* from

## TEANINICH

*distillery.* Founded in 1817 in the *Ross–shire* town of ALNESS, the *distillery* is now one of the largest in *Scotland.* TEANINICH is an assertive *single MALT WHISKY* with a *spicy, & smoky, satisfying* taste.

AGED **10** YEARS

43% vol   Distilled & Bottled in SCOTLAND. TEANINICH DISTILLERY, Alness.Ross-shire,Scotland.   70cl

**TEANINICH 10-year-old, 43 vol, Flora and Fauna**

| | |
|---|---|
| **Colour** Pale gold. | |
| **Nose** Aromatic. Fruity, leafy, smoky. | |
| **Body** Medium, rich. | |
| **Palate** Fruity, remarkably leafy, lightly peaty. Very appetising. | |
| **Finish** Leafy, herbal, complex flavours. Very appetising. | |

SCORE 74

**TEANINICH 17-year-old, 43 vol, Master of Malt**

**Colour** Pale gold.

**Nose** Herbal, leafy, slightly woody.

**Body** Medium.

**Palate** Herbal, earthy.

**Finish** Herbal, earthy, hint of peat.

SCORE 72

**TEANINICH 1982, 40 vol, Connoisseurs Choice**

**Colour** Full gold to bronze.

**Nose** Earthy, warm.

**Body** Medium, chewy.

**Palate** Creamy, earthy, toffeeish, spicy.

**Finish** Perfumy, sweet, then tart.

SCORE 76

# TOBERMORY

**Producer** Burn Stewart
**Region** Highlands  **Island** Mull

I F THE ART OF DISTILLATION was brought from Ireland over the Giant's Causeway, it must have arrived on Mull. The island's distillery traces its history to 1798, but it has operated only sporadically. In 1990, it reopened after a decade's silence, and later began to welcome visitors. It was acquired by Burn Stewart in 1993.

Over the years, it has continued to market a product called Tobermory, The Malt Scotch Whisky. This is a vatted malt, containing some Tobermory whiskies of up to 20 years old and proportions of younger whiskies from elsewhere. It has also marketed a blended Scotch, clearly identified on the label.

The distillery, in the town of Tobermory, was in the past known as Ledaig. Single malt whisky from the distillery has been bottled under that name by several independents. The Ledaig bottlings have a distinct island character. How strongly the island character will survive in the future is open to question. The water used by the distillery is very peaty, but the malt now being employed is unpeated. The new owners want to sell their new make for blending and they feel there is little demand in that department for heavily peated whiskies.

**House style** Faint peat, minty, sweet. Restorative.

*With the growing interest in malts, the Tobermory distillery, on the coast of Mull, is becoming a tourist attraction.*

**TOBERMORY, no age statement, 40 vol**

Colour Full gold.

Nose Light. Touch of peat. Some sweetness.

Body Light to medium. Smooth.

Palate Faint peat. Some malty dryness. Toffeeish notes.

Finish Light, soft, becoming sweeter.

SCORE 67

**LEDAIG, no age statement, Burn Stewart**

Colour Deeper gold.

Nose Lightly spicy and sweet.

Body Fuller, oilier.

Palate Hint of burnt grass. Slightly toasty. Touch of caramel.
Malty, spicy, minty.

Finish Very minty.

SCORE 71

**LEDAIG 18-year-old, 55.2 vol, James MacArthur**

Colour Pale gold.

Nose Intense iodine, seaweed.

Body Medium, firm.

Palate Peppery, spicy, seaweedy, dry.

Finish Peppery.

SCORE 79

**LEDAIG 1973, 40 vol, Gordon and MacPhail**

**Colour** Amber-red.

**Nose** Intensely peaty.

**Body** Medium, firm.

**Palate** Peaty, phenolic, dry, intense. An excellent island malt.

**Finish** Powerful, peaty, peppery, warming, lingering.

SCORE 76

**Other versions of Tobermory**
The Scotch Malt Whisky Society found a leathery peatiness in a
10-year-old at 60.2 vol, but this was much smoother and sweeter.
SCORE 75

# TOMATIN

**Producer** Takara, Shuzo and Okura
**Region** Highlands   **District** Speyside (Findhorn)

T HE FIRST SCOTTISH distillery to be wholly owned by a Japanese company. A second Japanese company subsequently acquired Ben Nevis, and others have shareholdings in Scottish whisky companies.

Tomatin was established in 1897, but saw its great years of expansion between the 1950s and the 1970s. During this period, it became the biggest malt distillery in Scotland. It is just a little smaller than Suntory's Hakushu distillery.

As a large distillery, Tomatin produced a broad-shouldered malt as a filler for countless blends during the boom years. It is neither the most complex nor the most assertive of malts, but it is far tastier than is widely realised. For the novice wishing to move from lighter single malts to something a little more imposing, the climb to Tomatin is well worthwhile.

**House style** Malty, spicy, rich. Restorative or after dinner.

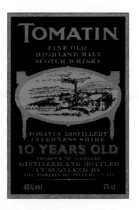

| TOMATIN 10-year-old, 40 vol |
| --- |
| **Colour** Full gold. |
| **Nose** Appetisingly fresh and clean, with a light, malty sweetness, and a hint of dry, perfumy smokiness. |
| **Body** Medium, soft, smooth. |
| **Palate** Sweet, but not overpoweringly so. Developing some gingery, perfumy dryness. |
| **Finish** Slightly chewy. |

SCORE 75

### TOMATIN 12-year-old, 43 vol

**Colour** Bronze.

**Nose** Malty, heathery, perfumy.

**Body** Medium to full. Soft, enwrapping.

**Palate** Clean, sweet, beautifully rounded. Tightly combined flavours. Spicy notes developing. Ginger.

**Finish** Soothing, warming. Long.

**SCORE 76**

### TOMATIN 13-year-old, 60.4 vol, Cadenhead

**Colour** Greeny-gold.

**Nose** Fresh, slightly sharp.

**Body** Medium, soft.

**Palate** Sweet, toffeeish.

**Finish** Perfumy, dry.

**SCORE 74**

### TOMATIN, 25-year-old, 43 vol

**Colour** Reddish-bronze.

**Nose** Malty, spicy (one taster found bergamot), soft fruitiness, oily, rounded.

**Body** Medium to full, smooth, firm.

**Palate** Rich, malty, spicy, toffeeish, moving to very lively, gingery spiciness.

**Finish** A crescendo of spiciness.

**SCORE 78**

### TOMATIN 1968, 40 vol, Connoisseurs Choice

**Colour** Full gold.

**Nose** Sweetish, malty, aromatic.

**Body** Medium, soft, lightly syrupy.

**Palate** Sweet, perfumy, fruity (orangey?).

**Finish** Rather quick.

### SCORE 75

### TOMATIN 1966, 43 vol, Signatory

**Colour** Bronze.

**Nose** Sweetish, malty, very aromatic.

**Body** Medium, soft, lightly syrupy.

**Palate** Sweetish, perfumy, toffeeish.

**Finish** Clinging toffee character.

### SCORE 75

### Other versions of Tomatin

A Gordon and MacPhail 1964 vintage at 40 vol is very dry – and notably fruity, especially in the nose. SCORE 74.

# TOMINTOUL

**Producer** Whyte and Mackay
**Region** Highlands   **District** Speyside (Livet)

THE VILLAGE OF TOMINTOUL (pronounced "tom in t'owl") is the base camp for climbers and walkers in the area around the Rivers Avon and Livet. Nearby, Cromdale and the Ladder Hills foreshadow the Cairngorm Mountains. This is the high, remote Livet countryside that once abounded in illicit distilleries. Tomintoul itself had a good few.

It is a few miles from the village to the present distillery, which is on the edge of forest, close to the Avon but still within the parish of Glenlivet. The distillery was built in the 1960s and is modern in appearance. Despite the wildness of the surroundings, the Livet malts are all characteristically elegant, and Tomintoul is very much in this style. In palate, Tomintoul is the lightest of the district's malts, although it has a little more body than its neighbour and rival Tamnavulin.

**House style** Delicate, grassy, perfumy. Aperitif.

| TOMINTOUL 12-year-old, 43 vol |
| :--- |
| **Colour** Full gold. |
| **Nose** Delicate, slightly spirity, grassy, perfumy. |
| **Body** Light, soft, smooth. |
| **Palate** Sweetish, notes of crushed barley, and maltiness. |
| **Finish** Lively and long-lasting. |

SCORE 76

# TORMORE

**Producer** Allied Distillers
**Region** Highlands **District** Speyside

**A**RCHITECTURALLY THE MOST elegant of all malt distilleries, and with a whisky of equal urbanity. As the hills around the Livet and Avon recede, Tormore presents a sight that is hard to believe. With its ornamental curling lake and fountains, its pristine, white buildings, decorative dormer windows, belfry and musical clock, the topiary, and the huge hill of dense firs forming a backdrop, Tormore might be a spa, offering a mountain water cure. Instead, it brings forth the water of life, *uisge beatha*. In its high, cold location, shaded from the sun, it produces a beautifully clean malt.

Tormore was erected in 1958, during the boom years for the Scotch whisky industry. It was the first completely new malt distillery to be built in the Highlands in the 20th century, and was evidently intended as a showpiece. It was built by Long John Distillers, and designed by Sir Albert Richardson.

**House style** Nutty, soft. Versatile.

### TORMORE 5-year-old, 43 vol

| | |
|---|---|
| **Colour** Full gold. | |
| **Nose** Clean, dry, faintly smoky. Toasted almonds? | |
| **Body** Medium, firm. | |
| **Palate** Appetising. Teasing balance of clean, malty sweetness and faintly smoky dryness. Leans slightly towards sweetness. | |
| **Finish** Smooth, very mellow for its youth. | |

**SCORE 75**

## TORMORE 10-year-old, 40 vol

**Colour** Full gold.

**Nose** Slightly more almondy.

**Body** Medium, smooth, with full texture.

**Palate** Soft, beautifully balanced.

**Finish** Soft, well-rounded and very long.

**SCORE 76**

# TULLIBARDINE

**Producer** Invergordon
**Region** Highlands    **District** Midlands

PRODUCT OF SCOTLAND

## Tullibardine

SINGLE HIGHLAND MALT
SCOTCH WHISKY

*A Single Malt Scotch Whisky of quality
and distinction distilled and bottled by*
TULLIBARDINE DISTILLERY LIMITED
BLACKFORD    PERTHSHIRE    SCOTLAND

40%vol                    70cl

**S**OUTH OF PERTH and halfway to Stirling, this is a southerly distillery, but still north of the Highland line. The location, Blackford, is noted for its well-water, and once produced famous ales. Tullibardine is available as a bottled single malt under the distillery label. The principal bottling is a 10-year-old, although there has also been a "Stillman's Dram" edition at 25 years old. This was winier, with spicy notes, including ginger. Its flavours were tightly combined, and gradually revealed many subtleties. Tullibardine is not especially well known, but in its own mild-mannered way it makes a pleasant pre-dinner companion.

**House style** Winey, fragrant. Aperitif.

| TULLIBARDINE 10-year-old, 40 vol |
| --- |
| **Colour** Gold. |
| **Nose** Soft, malty, sweetish. |
| **Body** Medium, firm, smooth. |
| **Palate** Full, with clean, grassy-malty sweetness. Only medium-sweet. Develops to a fruity, almost Chardonnay-like wineyness. |
| **Finish** Sweetish, fragrant, appetising, big. |

SCORE 76

# SINGLE GRAIN WHISKIES

A review of malts cannot include single grain whiskies, which are another species, but they merit an appendix. These two types of whisky do, after all, live together in a married state in every bottle of blended Scotch. While the malts provide the fullness of character in the blend, there is usually more grain whisky in the bottle.

Because it is made in a continuous process, in a column-shaped still, grain whisky can be produced more quickly and cheaply. It has less character, but it still takes some flavour from its principal raw material, whether unmalted barley, wheat or corn (maize). It is a whisky, not a neutral spirit, and it is aged for at least three years. There are eight grain distilleries operating in Scotland, and one or two more that are silent.

For decades, *United Distillers* and its predecessor *Distillers Company Limited* have bottled as a single grain the product of its Cameronbridge Distillery, in Fife. This is made available (but not actively marketed) as Cameron Brig, with no age statement, over the Haig name. It has an amber colour and hints of sherry and caramel to round out the grainy palate. In more recent years, a single grain from *Invergordon* distillery in the Northern Highlands has been actively marketed, at 10 and 22 years old, by the company of the same name. The design of the label and the advertising suggest that this is aimed at fashion-conscious young drinkers, perhaps in the worthy hope of weaning them off vodka.

There have been several independent bottlings of much older single grains. *Signatory* has a perfumy, woody, quite full, single grain from Dumbarton, and a sweeter one from North British. *James MacArthur* has a woody, sherryish Carsebridge, and softer, rounder examples from Ben Nevis and Lochside. These are bottlings for the lover of esoteric drinks.

*The Invergordon Single Grain has a golden colour and a soft, clean, sweetish palate.*

# VATTED MALTS

Why produce a whisky that is neither a single malt nor altogether a blend? It is argued that, while a single may vary according to vintage or season, a vatted malt can be more consistent. Are lovers of malts afflicted by an obsession with consistency? Perhaps the idea is attractive to importers, distributors or retailers who want their own malt label. At one point the vatted product was perhaps also seen as an introductory step into the world of malts. Today, with the growing popularity of the singles, less is heard of vatted malts.

The best-known vatted malt is probably *Strathconon* 12-year-old, produced under the Buchanan label by United Distillers. This is described as being vatted from four malts, chosen "one for bouquet, another for flavour, a third for body, the last for its ability to blend all four into a balanced, mellow, flavour." It has a bright, full, gold colour; an appetising, clean, malty-fruity nose; a soft, medium body; a dry, malty palate; and a dry finish. A very pleasant malt.

Another example from United Distillers, this time under the Haig label, is *Glenleven.* This is identified as a Highland malt, and said to be vatted from six singles. It has a fuller, bronze colour, a hint of peat in its spicy nose; a light to medium, slightly oily body; a malty-smoky palate, and a big, warming, long, dry finish. Quite a characterful whisky.

Where a distillery has ceased to operate, it may keep its label alive by producing a vatted malt. This is true of Glen Flagler. This was a Lowland single malt produced at Moffat, near Airdrie, in the mid-1960s and 1970s. In the mid-1980s the distillery was dismantled, but the label has been continued on a vatted malt. For the moment a proportion of the light-bodied Glen Flagler single malt is being used in the fuller-tasting vatted product. The vatted product, *Glen Flagler Pure Malt Special Reserve,* has a gold colour; both dryness and sweetness in the nose; a soft, sticky body; a sweetish palate; and a slightly resiny finish.

The best use of the vatted malt is that devised by Gordon and MacPhail. Among an interesting range of its own vattings, this company has a series, principally at 12 years old, devoted to some of the classic regions and districts, see opposite.

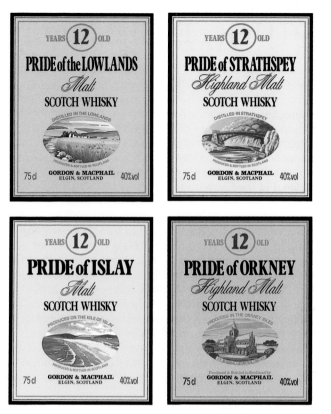

### PRIDE OF THE LOWLANDS
This has an amber colour; a lightly smoky nose (a dash of Glenkinchie?); a light, soft, smooth body; a sweetish, aromatic (a hint of grassiness, or linseed?) palate; and some sherry in the finish. Almost too characterful for today's Lowland selection.

### PRIDE OF STRATHSPEY
This standard 12-year-old has an amber colour; a hint of flowering currant in the nose; a medium to full body; a sweet, sherryish palate; and a smooth, malty finish. A 25-year-old *Pride of Strathspey* has a slightly fuller colour; a firmer body; a drier nose, with a hint of smokiness; more smokiness in the palate; and a dry, smoky finish.

### PRIDE OF ISLAY
A product that has a fairly full amber colour; light to medium peatiness in the nose; a medium to full body; some iodine and sappiness in the palate; and a long, peaty, dry sherryish finish. Very dry and assertive.

### PRIDE OF ORKNEY
This has an amber-red colour; a heather-honey nose; a medium-to-full, smooth body; a complex, heathery, peaty palate; and a long, warming, dryish finish.

# OTHER SINGLE MALTS

Several unlikely countries have released malt whiskies, though not singles. These whiskies have usually been distilled in Scotland and perhaps vatted in the country of "production".

Examples range from a herbal-tasting "Welsh" whisky to a malt called *Pride of India*. The latter, marketed by a company in Bangalore, bears the legend "distilled from the finest malt and blended with the choicest whiskies by Scotch experts". This product is lightly malty and sweetish, and falls away somewhat in the finish.

A country heavily settled by Scots – New Zealand – has a single malt called *Lammerlaw*, made in Dunedin (an old name for Edinburgh). There is said to have been whisky-making in Dunedin in the mid- and late 1800s, but the present distillery dates from 1968. *Lammerlaw* is said to be made from snow-melt and spring water from the Lammerlaw Mountains, and from New Zealand barley (which is of excellent quality), in pot-stills. The whisky has a sunny, golden colour; an intense but soft, pleasant, fruity aroma (apricot?); a light but firm body; more fruit in the palate; and a crisp, gingery, dry (faintly peaty) finish.

Two countries with a more vigorous tradition of whisky-distilling, Ireland and Japan, are also taking a greater interest in single malts.

## IRELAND

The newest single malt in Ireland is *Tyrconnell*, distilled at Cooley, near the Mountains of Mourne. This whiskey, made in 1989 and released in 1993, is gold in colour; with a cereal-grain aroma; a light body; an oily palate; and a very dry finish. With longer in the cask, it should make a pleasant malt, although there has been some question over the future of the distillery – the only independent whiskey-maker in Ireland.

The oldest malt in Ireland, from the long-silent Coleraine distillery, was released in 1993–94, at 34 years. This has a greenish tinge; a soft, almost fluffy aroma; a full body, with a slightly gritty texture; a toffeeish, spicy palate; and some woodiness in the finish. Coleraine was latterly owned by Irish Distillers, which also has Bushmills.

*Bushmills Malt*, at 10 years old, from County Antrim, Ireland, has a full gold colour; a warm, sweet nose, with some linseed; a very soft body; a sweetish, oily, malty palate; and a soft, smooth, dryish finish. Surprisingly, it has less of

*Home of the single-malt Irish whiskey, Bushmills Distillery, with its pagodas reflected in its dams, is a distinctive landmark.*

an obvious sherry character than its deluxe blend partner, *Black Bush*. These whiskeys, and the regular *Old Bushmills*, are triple-distilled. The Bushmills distillery, in the little town of the same name, was licensed by King James I in 1608. It is the world's oldest licensed malt distillery, though its single was only launched in the mid-1980s.

# JAPAN

The Japanese malt distilleries also began to bottle single malts during the 1980s. The best-known example is produced at Suntory's oldest distillery, Yamazaki, founded in 1923, between Osaka and Kyoto. *Yamazaki Pure Malt Whisky* has a pale colour; a fresh, clean, malty nose; a light to medium body; a crisp, dry, malty palate; and a long, soft, malty, warming finish. The company also has a larger distillery at Hakushu, and a smaller one, Hakushu East.

In 1992, Suntory launched two interesting new malts. One, called *Kioke Jikomi*, is distilled at the Hakushu East distillery. Its Japanese name is a reference to the use of wooden fermentation vessels. It is intended to have quite a full mouth feel, a robust palate, and some sherry character. I find it dry on the nose, with a good hint of peat; rounded in body; malty and sweetish in palate; and perfumy in finish. The other, called *Kodaru*, vats malts from Yamazaki and the big, main Hakushu distillery. This whisky is filtered through charcoal made from bamboo. There does seem to be a hint of ash on the nose, and I find the whisky light in body; sweet and Bourbon-like in palate; with a long, warming finish.

A second Japanese single malt is made by the smaller company Sanraku Ocean, at a tiny, pretty, overgrown, distillery founded in the 1930s in the mountain resort of Karuizawa, after which it takes its name. *Karuizawa Malt Whisky* has a pale colour; a sherryish nose; a light, slightly oily body; a clean, malty, sweet palate; and a crisp finish.

The newest entrant from Japan, *Nikka "Hokkaido" Single Malt*, has an amber-red colour; a dry nose; a medium to full body; a dry, malty, sherryish palate, with some chewiness; and a very smooth, mild, sweetish finish. This distinctive malt is produced at Nikka's oldest distillery, on the island of Hokkaido. The founder of Nikka studied on Speyside from 1918, and the small distillery, in the seaside town of Yoichi, is a handsome tribute to its inspirations.

*The distinctive rooftops and stone buildings of the Nikka distillery.*

*Hakushu is the largest malt distillery in the world.*

# STORING AND SERVING SINGLE MALTS

Malt whisky is a drink to contemplate, and certainly not one to rush. As with fine wine, the way a malt is served can add to or detract from the enjoyment of drinking it. To make sure malts are enjoyed to the full, therefore, it is worth bearing in mind a few points, which I have outlined below.

### Temperature

A malt in its natural state will throw an unattractive haze if it is refrigerated. That is why the commercial versions are filtered at cold temperatures. This chill-filtration removes solids that might otherwise precipitate – but also strips out some texture and taste. There is no reason to store malts at low temperatures, and every reason to avoid chilling them or adding ice. Cold numbs the tongue, and ice brings about changes in the malt. Whisky most fully expresses itself if it is stored and served at room temperature. A single malt is not meant to be a cold, thirst-quenching drink.

### Glassware

With its no-nonsense shape, and refraction of the light through the colours of the drink, the traditional cut-glass tumbler is aesthetically pleasing. Where it fails is in presenting the colour naturally, and – more importantly – in retaining the aroma. These two requirements favour the use of a brandy-type "snifter glass" for single malts, and this is becoming more popular. Whisky blenders do their tasting in a similar glass designed for their purpose. It is in the style of a tall, narrow snifter or an elongated sherry copita.

### Dilution

The texture – but not necessarily the aroma and palate – of the fuller-bodied style of the malt is best appreciated if it is sampled undiluted. A good compromise is to add just the odd drop of water, "like the dew on a rose", in the words of whisky-merchant and writer Wallace Milroy. A small amount of water will help awaken the bouquet of a malt, and bring out aromatics in the palate. Some professional blenders work only with their nose, not finding it necessary to let the whisky pass their lips. Others like to sample the whisky undiluted, though this can soon anaesthetise the palate. Some blenders like to dilute 50-50, using distilled or very pure water.

# VISITING
# THE DISTILLERIES

There was a time when many malt distilleries did not even have a bottle of their product on the premises, or a licence to offer a glass to visitors. However, as interest in single malts has grown, so has the number of distilleries that are formally organised to welcome visitors. Many now have what they call visitor reception centres, sometimes showing a video on the production process, almost always offering a guided tour, usually with a tasting at the end, perhaps with a gift-shop, and sometimes a bar or restaurant. Even distilleries that do not formally offer tours will often welcome visitors.

A number of well-known Highland distilleries with reception centres have organised themselves into a "Malt Whisky Trail" for the benefit of visitors. A booklet and map can be obtained from the Scottish Tourist Board, at 23 Ravelstone Terrace, Edinburgh (tel: 031 332 2433) and some other Scottish tourist offices.

Visitors to Edinburgh can view the history of the industry from the comfort of a motorised cask at The Scotch Whisky Heritage Centre, at 354 Castlehill, on the Royal Mile, Edinburgh. The Cairngorm Whisky Centre and Museum (tel: 0479 810574) is in Aviemore, Scotland's main skiing centre. Visitors who would like to wander freely in a perfectly preserved, unmodernised distillery should see Dallas Dhu, near Forres (Information: Historic Scotland, 20 Brandon Street, Edinburgh, tel: 031 244 3101).

The following distilleries are willing to show visitors around. Some of them have reception centres and shops, but many are ordinary working distilleries and a telephone call in advance is advisable. The usual opening hours are 9.30 am to 4 pm, Monday to Friday. Some distilleries are open all year round; others are only open in the summer months.

ABERFELDY
Aberfeldy, Perthshire
0887 820330
(Visitors' centre)

ABERLOUR
Aberlour, Banffshire
0340 871204
(Visitors' centre)

AUCHROISK
Mulben, Banffshire
0542 860333

AULTMORE
Keith, Banffshire
0542 882762

BALBLAIR
Edderton, Ross-shire
0862 82273

BALMENACH
Cromdale, Grantown-on-Spey,
Morayshire
0479 872569

BEN NEVIS
Fort William, Inverness-shire,
0397 702476
(Visitors' centre)

BENRIACH
Longmorn, Elgin, Morayshire
0542 887471

BENRINNES
Aberlour, Banffshire
0340 871215

BLADNOCH
Bladnoch, Wigtownshire
0988 402235
(Visitors' centre)

BLAIR ATHOL
Pitlochry, Perthshire
0796 472234
(Visitors' centre)

BOWMORE
Bowmore, Islay, Argyll
0496 810441
(Visitors' centre)

BRUICHLADDICH
Bruichladdich, Islay, Argyll
0496 810221
(Visitors' centre)

BUNNAHABHAIN
Port Askaig, Islay, Argyll
0496 840646

CAOL ILA
Port Askaig, lslay, Argyll
0496 840207
(Visitors' centre)

CARDHU
Cardhu, Morayshire
0340 810204
(Visitors' centre)

CLYNELISH
Brora, Sutherland
0408 621444
(Visitors' centre)

CRAGGANMORE
Ballindalloch, Banffshire
0807 500202

CRAIGELLACHIE
Craigellachie, Banffshire
0340 881212/881228

DAILUAINE
Carron, Aberlour, Banffshire
0340 810361/810362

DALLAS DHU (not in production)
Forres, Morayshire
0309 676548
(Visitors' centre)

DALMORE
Alness, Rothshire
0349 882362

DALWHINNIE
Dalwhinnie, Inverness-shire
0528 522264

DUFFTOWN
Dufftown, Keith, Banffshire
0340 820224/820773

EDRADOUR
Pitlochry, Perthshire
0796 472095
(Visitors' centre)

FETTERCAIRN
Fettercairn, Kincardineshire
0561 340244
(Visitors' centre)

GLENALLACHIE
Aberlour, Banffshire
0340 871315

GLENBURGIE
Forres, Morayshire
0343 85258

GLENCADAM
Brechin, Angus
0356 622217

GLENRONACH
Forgue, by Huntly,
Aberdeenshire
0466 82346
(Visitors' centre)

GLENDULLAN
Dufftown, Banffshire
0340 820250

GLEN ELGIN
Longmorn, Morayshire
0343 86212
(Visitors' centre)

GLENFARCLAS
Marypark, Ballindalloch,
Banffshire
0807 500257
(Visitors' centre)

GLENFIDDICH
Dufftown, Banffshire
0340 820373
(Visitors' centre)

GLENGOYNE
Dumgoyne, Stirlingshire
041 242 5300
(Visitors' centre)

GLEN GRANT
Rothes, Morayshire
0542 887471
(Visitors' centre)

GLENKINCHIE
Pencaitland, Tranent,
East Lothian
0875 340333
(Visitors' centre)

THE GLENLIVET
Minmore, Banffshire
0542 887471
(Visitors' centre)

GLENLOSSIE
By Elgin, Morayshire
0343 86331

GLENMORANGIE
Tain, Ross-shire
0862 892043

GLEN MORAY
Elgin, Morayshire
0343 542577

GLEN ORD
Muir of Ord, Ross-shire
0463 870421
(Visitors' centre)

GLEN SCOTIA
Campbeltown, Argyll
0586 552288

GLEN SPEY
Rothes, Morayshire
0542 860333

GLENTURRET
Crieff, Perthshire
0764 652424
(Visitors' centre)

HIGHLAND PARK
Kirkwall, Orkney
0856 873107
(Visitors' centre)

INCHGOWER
Buckie, Banffshire
0542 831161

INVERLEVEN
Dumbarton, Dumbartonshire
0389 65111

JURA
Craighouse, Jura, Argyll
0496 82240

KNOCKANDO
Knockando, Morayshire
0542 860333

KNOCKDHU
Knock, Banffshire
0466 86223

LAGAVULIN
Port Ellen, Islay, Argyll
0496 302250/302400
(Visitors' centre)

LAPHROAIG
Port Ellen, Islay, Argyll
0496 302418
(Visitors' centre)

LINKWOOD
Elgin, Morayshire
0343 547004

LOCHNAGAR
Crathie, Ballater,
Aberdeenshire
0339 742273
(Visitors' centre)

LOCHSIDE
Montrose, Tayside
0674 672737

THE MACALLAN
Craigellachie, Banffshire
0340 871471

MILTONDUFF
Elgin, Morayshire
0343 547433

MORTLACH
Dufftown, Keith, Banffshire
0340 820318

OBAN
Stafford Street, Oban, Argyll
0631 62110
(Visitors' centre)

ORD *See Glen Ord*

PITTYVAICH
Dufftown, Keith, Banffshire
0340 820561

PULTENEY
Wick, Caithness
0955 2371

ROSEBANK
Falkirk, Stirlingshire
0324 623325

SCAPA
Kirkwall, Orkney
0856 872071

SINGLETON OF AUCHROISK
*See Auchroisk*

SPEYBURN
Rothes, Morayshire
0340 831213

STRATHISLA
Keith, Banffshire
0542 887471
(Visitors' centre)

STRATHMILL
Keith, Banffshire
0542 22295

TALISKER
Carbost, Isle of Skye
0478 640203

TAMDHU
Knockando, Morayshire
0340 810221
(Visitors' centre)

TAMNAVULIN
Ballindalloch, Dumbartonshire
0807 590442
(Visitors' centre)

TOBERMORY
Tobermory, Isle of Mull
0688 2647

TOMATIN
Tomatin, Inverness-shire
0808 2234
(Visitors' centre)

TORMORE
Grantown-on-Spey, Morayshire
0807 510244

TULLIBARDINE
Blackford, Perthshire
0764 682252

# INDEX

# FURTHER READING

The World Guide to Whisky
*Michael Jackson* (1993, 1991, 1987)

Scotch Missed
*Brian Townsend* (1993)

The Whisky Trails
*Gordon Brown* (1993)

A Taste of Scotch
*Derek Cooper* (1989)

Whisky and Scotland
*Neil M Gunn* (1988, 1977, 1935)

The whiskies of Scotland
*R J S McDowall*, revised by
*William Waugh* (1986, 1967)

The Schweppes Guide to
Scotch *Philip Morrice* (1983)

Whisky *Gavin D Smith* (1993)

The Making of Scotch Whisky
*Michael Moss and John Hume*
(1981)

**Earlier Classics**

Scotch Whisky *David Daiches*

Scotch
*Sir Robert Bruce Lockhart*

The Whisky Distilleries
of the United Kingdom
*Alfred Barnard*

# ACKNOWLEDGMENTS

My thanks again to all the people whose assistance was acknowledged in the first and second editions of this book, and to the following: Dr Jim Swan, of Tatlock and Thomson, Analytic Chemists, Glasgow; Sabina Bruning and many colleagues at United Distillers; Sylvia Corrieri, Allied Distillers; Jill Preston and Libby Jones, Chivas and Glenlivet; Trevor Cowan, Invergordon; Jacqui Stacey, Inver House; Jim Turle, Lang Brothers; Robin Dods, Burn Stewart; Loraine Morris, Justerini and Brooks; Lesley Young and colleagues, Glenmorangie; D. A. Eames, Tomatin; Alex W. Ross, Ben Nevis Distillery; I. M. Phillips, William Lawson. Countless other people in the industry have helped me over the years, and their assistance is much appreciated.

**Dorling Kindersley** would like to thank Melissa Denny of Diptych for editing and designing the first edition of this book. Many thanks also to Karen Ward and Alison Verity for design assistance in the third edition, and to Catherine Toqué for production.

**Photography** by Ian Howes, except title page, Stephen Oliver; page 12, bottom left, Glenmorangie Distillery Ltd.; page 14, Glenturret; page 96, Campbell Distillers Ltd.; and page 262, Tetsuya Fukui. Extra label photography by Steve Gorton.

**Maps** produced by Lovell Johns Limited, Oxford.

**Typeset** in ITC Garamond.

**Reproduction** by Colourscan, Singapore.